THE TRAIN DOESN'T STOP IN WAGNER, MONTANA ANYMORE AND NEITHER DO I

Travels in America

Joe Kelly

Joe Kelly writes a newspaper column in Utica, NY for the Observer-Dispatch. He began work at the O-D in 1976 and has written a column since 1984. His column appears five times a week, and he does a daily commentary on radio station WIBX. He is the assistant director of the Boilermaker Road Race. He is married and lives in New Hartford.

Good Times Publishing
P.O. Box 4545
Utica, NY 13504

Also by Joe Kelly

Utica Sesquicentennial Scrapbook

Joe Kelly's Greatest Ever Little Trivia Book

Joe Kelly's Travel Book

Portions of this book were originally published in the Observer-Dispatch, some in a slightly different form. Permission from the Observer-Dispatch to reprint them here is gratefully acknowledged.

Cover photo by Al Gorney, President of the Utica and Mohawk Valley Chapter of the National Railway Historical Society

ISBN 0-9639290-1-1

Library of Congress Cataloging-in-Publication Data

Kelly, Joe, 1946-
The train doesn't stop in Wagner, Montana, anymore and neither do I : travels in America / Joe Kelly

1. United States - Description and travel. 2. Amtrak.
3.Railroad travel - United States. I. Title
E169.04K45 1995
917.304'929-dc20 94-39152
CIP

Printed in Yorkville, NY by Vicks Lithograph & Printing Corporation

This book is dedicated to Joseph Brian Miner, my grandson.

Acknowledgements

Portions of this book originally appeared in the Observer-Dispatch, some in a slightly different form, and I thank editor Rick Jensen and the newspaper for giving permission to publish them here.

"It sounds like a worthy project," Jensen said.

I hope he is right.

Speaking of the O-D, Nancy Smeltzer, Jack Marsh and John McMillan all helped in one way or another.

Amtrak's Pat Kelly helped with scheduling and advice on several trips. Once, she interrupted her busy schedule to show me around the Washington, D.C. train station, and we aren't even related.

Al Gorney took the cover photograph. Missy Brindisi typed. And Dana Jerrard and the folks at Vicks Lithograph & Printing produced the book. Working with all of them was a pleasure.

Cindy and Brian Miner and Alan and Jackie Serley helped in a variety of ways.

The biggest help came from Kathy Kelly.

To all of them, I have two words: thank you.

Words, though, aren't enough to express my appreciation.

Introduction

You've probably never heard of Wagner, Montana. It is a small town, population 30, located along the Milk River, about 50 miles south of the Canadian border.

Milk is an appropriate name. Mineral deposits being swept into the river, which I've seen from the train, give it a milky appearance.

Wagner, which is near the eastern edge of the Fort Belknap Indian Reservation, has only a few homes. There isn't even a post office.

To get to Wagner, Montana from Utica, New York, take the Lake Shore Limited to Chicago and switch to the Empire Builder, a train that makes a daily run to Seattle. On the way, the Empire Builder goes through Illinois, Wisconsin, Minnesota, North Dakota and Montana.

The train makes a brief stop in Malta, Montana, about 15 miles east of Wagner. These days, that's as close as you can get by train.

The train stopped in Wagner in 1901, though, when Butch Cassidy and the Sundance Kid blew up the safe in the express car and rode away with $68,000.

If anything more exciting has ever happened in Wagner, it has escaped my attention.

I've never been on a train when it was being robbed. I have, however, been on trains that have broken down, trains that have made emergency stops, trains that have come through blizzards, trains that have passed through beautiful sunsets, sunrises and rainbows, and once I was on the California Zephyr when it was mooned by a group of female rafters on the Colorado River.

Binoculars are now an essential part of my luggage. You never know when you'll see a rainbow.

By the way, mooning the train is something the rafters -- men and women -- have done for years. Some rafters even strip down, stand up and wave as the train goes by.

There's something about a train. People can't resist waving.

When the Zephyr gets alongside that section of the Colorado River, passengers and crew crowd around the windows. After all, it would be impolite not to wave back to the rafters.

That's why I elbowed my way between two elderly women who got to the window before me. Say what you want about me, just don't ever say I'm impolite.

I didn't see any naked people on my first ever train trip, which was in the early 1950s. My grandparents took me to New York City. They couldn't wait to get there. I wanted to keep on riding.

Over the years I've ridden every long distance train Amtrak has to offer, some more than once. Three times I've ridden up front in the engine. Once I even got to blow the horn.

Traveling through America by train, visiting places, meeting people and seeing things is what this book is about. For the most part, the rides in this book were taken in the mid to late 1980s.

Most of the quotes used in the following stories are exact, or as exact as they can be when someone is talking fast and someone else is taking notes fast, trying to keep up.

In a few cases, I've reconstructed conversations after they took place. Pulling out a notebook while someone is talking isn't always the nicest or smartest thing to do. In those reconstructed conversations, the thrust of what was said is 100 percent accurate, even if every word between quotation marks isn't.

The sentence you are now reading is being written after midnight. The house is quiet. If I open the window, I'll be able to hear the horn of the westbound Lake Shore Limited when she pulls out of Utica's Union Station in a few minutes. It will remind me of how much there is to see in this country and how much I enjoy riding the train to get there.

But there's one community I'll never visit, because the train doesn't stop in Wagner, Montana anymore and neither do I.

Joe Kelly

Contents

Janice Hart

I met Janice Hart seven years ago, or maybe it was eight. It was the end of September, though. I remember because I had just celebrated my birthday.

She looked to be 40ish, which gave us something in common. She was waiting to board Amtrak's westbound Lake Shore Limited, which gave us something else in common.

She sat by herself in the middle of one of the long passenger benches, feet up on her suitcase, reading a paperback. She wore blue jeans, and a green and black plaid Pendelton over a white T-shirt.

There are eight of those long, wooden benches in Utica's Union Station, room enough to seat a few hundred. The station opened in 1914, when hundreds of people did, in fact, sit in the 15,000 square foot room waiting for trains.

In its prime, the station had three ticket windows, an information window, two shoeshine stands, a bar and grill, Western Union office, barbershop, Railway Express office and a dozen or so Red Caps to carry luggage.

Danny Creaco's barbershop remains, but his customers come in off the street, not off the train. You'll need to go elsewhere to eat, drink, or get a shine. And when it comes to luggage, you're on your own. As for telegrams, I'm not sure people send them anymore.

I've seen pictures of the station taken during World War II. People were shoulder to shoulder. Many of them were military people. The station even had a USO Club.

Which reminds me of the Bagg Memorial Building. The small building, just a few steps west of the train station, occupies the site of Bagg's Hotel.

The hotel was torn down without the aid of machinery because Mrs. Thomas Proctor, the owner, wanted to employ as many men as possible during the Great Depression.

When the site was cleared, Maria Proctor had the memorial building put up at a cost of $10,000, a not insignificant sum in 1932. Her idea was to commemorate the great history of Bagg's Hotel, which hosted guests the likes of General Lafayette, writer Charles Dickens and President U.S. Grant.

Mrs. Proctor's idea was to display the hotel's register and other memorabilia in the memorial building. That never happened, though. Someone ran off with the memorabilia.

Military police used the building during the war. What with thousands of soldiers and sailors coming and going through Union Station, M.P.s had to be close by.

I've been told that the Bagg building was also used as a place to distribute condoms to G.I.s. That might not be true, though.

At least the Bagg building got used for something during the war. That hasn't been the case for a long time.

Union Station changed after the war. Travelers took more to the sky and roads. Train stations such as Utica's became less and less crowded.

In fact, on that September night eight years ago, or maybe seven, only six of us, including Janice Hart, waited for the Lake Shore, which runs back and forth between New York City and Chicago.

It was a few minutes past midnight. The Lake Shore had departed New York City four and a half hours earlier and was scheduled to arrive in Utica in about 30 minutes, not a time most people would pick to start a trip.

I didn't mind, though. There was a bar at the station then and you could wait over a drink and listen to songs from the 1960s on the jukebox.

And when the train arrived, an Amtrak attendant escorted you to your sleeping compartment, where the bed would be turned down. Two small bottles of wine and snacks would be next to the pillow. Relaxing in bed as the lights of Central New York glide by is not such a bad way to start a trip.

Ms. Hart - I don't know if she was married - put down her spy novel, took her feet off the suitcase, removed her eyeglasses and spoke first.

"Where are you heading?"

That one question is responsible for starting thousands of conversations in airports and train stations everyday. I don't include bus stations because people there are usually grim faced and less inclined to chat.

"I'm going through to Chicago," I responded, "then San Francisco. How about you?"

"Chicago, then L. A."

She said she lived in New York City and had stopped in Utica to visit a friend. Now she was getting on with her vacation. She said she loved to travel.

"I hope the train isn't late," she added.

It wasn't.

I saw her again the next morning in the Lake Shore's packed dining car. As it turned out, we were both assigned to the same table for breakfast. She took my suggestion and ordered the railroad style French toast.

"There are basically three kinds of people in the world," she said and sipped from her cup of coffee, "those who love to travel, those who are forced to travel, and those who never travel."

I said I agreed.

"Which," she asked, "are you?"

"I'm in the first group."

I can't remember a time when I didn't get excited about taking a trip.

Over a second cup of dining car coffee, we talked about favorite places.

I asked, "If you could have a free ticket to anywhere, where would it be?"

She turned and looked out at the passing Ohio countryside and quoted something she had read years before. She said the words were permanently stuck in her mind.

"The place I enjoy visiting most," she said, "is the place I've never been."

We exchanged business cards that morning over breakfast. She sold real estate. If her jewelry was any indication, she sold a lot of real estate.

She was going to send me a postcard from Los Angeles. I was going to send her one from San Francisco.

She didn't. Neither did I.

We never saw or heard from each other again. That's usually the case when you meet someone while traveling, which, of course, is why people talk freely about their personal lives to complete strangers. Nothing said will come back to embarrass them or cause problems.

But I still think of what she said that morning in the Lake Shore's dining car. She was quite right, which is why I use those words when someone asks where I'd most like to visit.

"The place I enjoy visiting most," I tell them, "is the place I've never been."

Hitting The Road With Bare Essentials

Aboard the Lake Shore Limited -- Train travelers can give their bags to a station clerk who will have them put into the baggage car. Few passengers do this, however.

I once toured an Amtrak baggage car. It was almost empty.

Train travelers are like airplane travelers. They like their suitcases where they can touch them. Hand your bags over to some stranger and who knows when you'll see them again.

I have only one suitcase with me on this trip. I don't want to go traipsing around the country loaded down with bags.

The suitcase has lots of pockets and zippers and is small enough to fit snugly in the overhead rack of a day coach or to stow out of the way in a roomette, which is what Amtrak calls the sleeping compartment I've been assigned to.

But since it isn't a very big bag, decisions on what to bring and what to leave behind had to be made.

I've kept clothes to a minimum. I usually bring a bunch of clothes and end up not wearing most of them. Not this time.

Here are things I did pack:

- Alarm clock. They wake you on trains, but I want insurance. I don't want to wake up in Omaha when I should have gotten off in Chicago.

- Small flashlight. I was in Dodge City, Kansas once and the lights went out in the hotel where I was staying. I had a heck of a time getting out. When I got home, a kind person gave me a flashlight and said, "Don't ever travel without one." I no longer do.

- Shoes and clothes for running. One reason travel is so tiring, I believe, is that people sit for hours doing nothing. You have to exercise and get the blood moving.

- Postage stamps, envelopes, writing pad, pens, notebooks. There's no sense in going to great places if you don't write to people back home and make them jealous.

- A Walkman radio. Just because I enjoy going around the country on a train doesn't mean I want to miss what's going on in the world.

- First aid kit and family size bottle of aspirin. There's probably an old railroad saying that goes something like this: "The longer the trip, the more aspirin you'll need." If there isn't such a saying, there should be. Trust me.

- Books. I have Len Deighton's "Spy Hook" novel, which I bought months ago but haven't had time to read, and "Blue Highways," which is about someone who travels alone around the country, an appropriate book seeing as how I'm doing the same thing. One of the nice things about train travel is that it provides the time and atmosphere for the reading you can't get to at home.

- Sewing kit, the kind they give you in those expensive hotels. There's a needle, buttons and safety pins. I don't go anywhere without safety pins.

- Wash N Drys. There's something about traveling which causes your hands to get sticky more often than they would if you were at home. Why this is, I don't know. It's true, though.

- Extra business cards. On the road, many people end their conversations like this: "Let me give you my business card." It's no fun unless you have a business card, too.

- Map of the United States, Amtrak's route system map and a timetable. No train I've ever been on has gotten lost, which means it's only a matter of time until it happens.

- Sunglasses. Railroad cars are surprisingly sunny. Besides, wearing sunglasses discourages people from trying to start conversations. Believe me, there are times on the train when you don't feel like talking.

- Swiss Army Knife, the kind with all the attachments. My model has a corkscrew, can opener, bottle opener, two kinds of screwdrivers, tweezers, scissors, toothpick, magnifying glass, small blade and big blade. I believe my Swiss Army Knife also turns into a fishing pole, but I haven't figured it out yet.

- Binoculars, small enough to fit the palm of your hand. It's frustrating to sit in an observation car and see something off in the distance and not be able to make it out. And if you read the introduction to this book, you know what rafters on the Colorado River do when the train goes by. It's a sight to see. Binoculars help you see it better.

Nate Brawner

A ride on a train is like going to a restaurant. The meal might not always be the best, but if the service is really good you don't mind so much. Things go wrong on long distance trains, but Nate Brawner made you not mind so much.

There was something about his voice that long ago caught my attention. It was an older voice, mellow and soothing. And respectful.

I would hear the voice on the train's public address system each time I rode the Lake Shore Limited to New York City. I ride the Lake Shore whenever I can find a reason. I have a long list of reasons.

Ever see the "Blues Brothers"?

Cab Calloway, an orchestra leader and singer, is in the movie. Maybe it was my imagination, but Nate's voice on the train's public address system reminded me of Cab Calloway's.

"Thank you for riding with us," Nate's sincere voice would say.

Amtrak management insists, I am sure, that employees thank passengers, but there is no way they can insist it be done sincerely.

"It has been a pleasure serving you," Nate would say when making his announcements.

His voice made you believe it really had been.

"Please be careful getting off the train," he would say.

He had probably said those things thousands of times before, but there was nothing mechanical in his voice. He wasn't somebody going through the motions.

His voice also gave passengers information about the area the train was passing through, something that is supposed to be done on all Amtrak trains, but sometimes isn't. Nate never missed.

As I said, I listened and smiled at his voice for a long time. I suppose his voice is a small part of the train's operation, but it makes the trip much nicer.

I remember the first time I met Nate. I asked a conductor where I could find the man belonging to the voice on the train's public address system and was directed three cars ahead to the dining car. Nate sat in a booth filling out Amtrak forms.

I introduced myself and told him I had been listening to his voice for many years and that he made my trips pleasant. He smiled.

"Thank you, sir. That's very nice of you to say so."

He didn't look much like Cab Calloway.

Nate pushed his paperwork to one side and invited me to sit. The train was running alongside the Hudson River, which was busy with boaters.

Over the next several miles Nate told me about himself. He said he was married and would be 65 years old in a month. He said he had four children, 14 grandchildren, loved to bowl, and lived in Chicago, starting point for the Lake Shore.

He said he started railroading 43 years ago, working as a bus boy in the dining car.

"I refused to remain as a bus boy. I wanted to work my way up."

He did. He worked as waiter, dining car attendant and sleeping car porter. He is now in charge of all onboard services on the Lake Shore and is Amtrak's most senior man in that position.

"I've enjoyed this work. It has been good to me. It has been a wonderful life. I like people, you see, and that means a lot in this business."

Sometimes Nate looked out the window at the river as he talked. When he did that I had the feeling he was talking more to himself than me.

"I've never considered what I do to be menial work. It's important work. The passengers are buying a service and they've got a right to expect good service. If you don't give the service in the right tone and with the right attitude, you're defeating the whole purpose of your job."

I said he sounded sincere.

"I am. There are two ways of saying 'good morning.' You can say 'good morning' and mean it or you can say 'good morning' and make it sound like 'what the hell are you doing here,' if you know what I mean."

I said I knew exactly, and asked about the pin in his lapel.

"Well, sir, this is a service excellence pin," he said, taking it off so I could examine it. "I was awarded it three months ago. They called me in one day and presented it. Apparently a passenger wrote to Amtrak and said something about me. I was very flattered."

Nate excused himself and went back to his work. The last I saw of him was in Grand Central Station. Someone had left an article of clothing in the dining car and he was trying to find the owner.

By the way, I learned one other thing about Nate Brawner. He will retire next month. He said he would try to time his last trip so that it falls on September 23, his 65th birthday.

Train engineers have a nice retirement custom. On the engineer's last run, a group of retired engineers use their train passes and go along for the ride, a kind of honor guard.

And when they pull into the station at the end of the line and the engineer's career is finished, they all go have a party. Oftentimes, it involves having a beer. Sometimes even two.

I asked Nate if there would be anything like that for him. He said there would not. There was a time when employees got a gold railroad watch and a ceremony, he said, but that was long ago when railroads were many and airlines were few.

"The ending is a little chilly now," Nate said. "You turn in your equipment on the last day and you're done."

It might not be much, but I intend to be on Nate Brawner's last run, if only for a few miles. I will insist that he sit at a table in the dining car and do me the honor of allowing me to serve him coffee and birthday cake.

Nate's Last Trip

Aboard the Lake Shore Limited -- We were running east and parallel to the New York State Thruway. The Amtrak train wasn't yet up to speed. We were only a few minutes out of Utica's Union Station.

The train was crowded. It took those of us who got on at Utica time to find seats.

The Lake Shore originates in Chicago and goes to New York City. Chicago is where Nate Brawner lives when he isn't aboard the Lake Shore. He was my reason for being on the train.

He turned 65 a few days ago. This was his last trip. He would be in New York in five hours, have a leisurely lunch, head back to Chicago and it would be over. He would retire after 43 years on the railroad.

He started as a bus boy in the dining car and then became a porter, which involved shining shoes, pressing pants and brushing hats. He then worked up to lounge car attendant, waiter and supervisor. Now he is in charge of passenger services on the train.

I've listened to his voice on the train's public address system for years. He has made the same announcements thousands of times, but instead of boredom in his voice you hear concern and goodness. I wish you could hear him.

And there's something else. Nate always treated his passengers with respect and courtesy. I'll tell you what he told me once.

"I've never considered what I do to be menial work. It's important work. The passengers are buying a service and they've got a right to expect good service. If you don't give the service in the right tone and with the right attitude, you're defeating the whole purpose of your job."

When I let it be known that Nate was retiring, an interesting thing happened. People in Utica, Rome, New Hartford, and St. Johnsville sent me letters. They didn't know Nate Brawner by name, but they had ridden his train and knew about him from his public address system announcements.

"I frequently travel on Amtrak," a Utica woman wrote, "and as I sit and listen to the voice, it is assuring, friendly and professional. If the train is late, you soon forget the delay when you hear the pleasant voice assure you that all is well."

A woman from St. Johnsville, who said she was a bride when she rode on Nate's train in the 1950s, sent me a card and a retirement gift to give him.

As I said, the train was crowded. I started walking through the coaches trying to find him. I heard him before I saw him. He was making an announcement, telling passengers about the history of the Mohawk Valley.

When he finished, he said, "If I can assist you in any way, please let me know. I'd be happy to do so."

When I finally found him, he was waiting on tables in the dining car. There was a big breakfast crowd. I stood in the corner and watched him help the waiters. He looked like he was enjoying himself.

When the car emptied, we sat and talked. I told him I was surprised to see him waiting tables, which isn't a supervisor's job, especially on his last trip. If anyone had the right to take it easy on a trip, he did.

"Well, Mr. Kelly, I do it because it enhances service. I don't want people having to wait any longer than necessary. I don't mind. I enjoy the people."

I've given up trying to get him to call me by my first name.

I gave him the letters from people who had ridden his train. He read slowly.

He finished and said, "Well I'll be. I don't know how to express myself."

Maybe it was the sun coming through the window that made his eyes water.

"I've got to tell you something," he said.

He went on to tell me about a surprise party for him at the station just before the train left Chicago. A lot of people were there, including some Amtrak big shots who came in special to shake his hand.

"It was quite a thrill. I'm leaving on a high note. I had to call my wife and tell her. I didn't want to wait until I got back. It made me a little juicy eyed," which is Nate Brawner's way of saying the sun was in his eyes.

While the train sped to Albany, we talked about his career, which he has loved, and his feelings about leaving.

"I've done this for so many years. I've worked all my life. Even when I was a child, I hauled groceries. I don't know what it will be like to wake up in the morning and not have a job. It won't be as easy as I thought."

We talked about his first days on the railroad. He laughed and told me how embarrassed he was the time he spilled a drink on a woman. Instead of taking her glass, putting it on his tray and pouring, which was the proper procedure, he poured as she held the glass. The train rocked at the wrong time.

"I've told that story to people I've trained. I wanted to give them an example of how important it is to do things the right way."

And we talked about some of the railroad characters he worked with over the years, people like Paprika Bartlow, a cook.

"Whatever Paprika Bartlow prepared, he prepared using paprika. He used paprika on everything. I told him once, 'Paprika, not everybody likes paprika,' He told me, 'Well, they ought to,' and he kept using it."

Albany, where I would leave the train, was minutes away. The engineer must have driven faster than usual. I went back to my seat. Nate Brawner went back to work.

His voice came on the public address system. He thanked the passengers for riding Amtrak and said it had been an honor serving them.

He didn't say anything about it being his last trip. I wish he had.

A woman across the aisle from me was taken by the sincerity in Nate's voice, just as I have always been. The woman leaned over to her friend and said, "He sounds like he really means it."

I couldn't resist.

"He does ma'am," I said. "He really does."

Mister Brawner: He Was One in a Million

This will not be written nearly as well as I would like. Maybe I shouldn't even be writing now. Maybe I should wait until there is more time. I don't know.

I do know I feel better sometimes when I get things down on paper. It's a kind of therapy. And I know that many people are interested in Nate Brawner, a good and gentle man, and would want to know what has happened to him as soon as possible.

I just hung up the telephone. The caller identified himself as Kenny Brawner of New York City. Kenny is Nate's brother.

Nate worked on the Lake Shore Limited. That's how we got to be friendly.

He rode the train from Chicago to New York City and back again for years. His job was to take care of the passengers, which he did quite nicely.

He considered his job the most important one on the railroad and conducted himself accordingly. A passenger wasn't going to have a bad experience on his train, not if Nate Brawner had anything to say about it.

He was a supervisor, but you'd still see him waiting on tables when the dining car got busy or getting a pillow if somebody looked like they could use one. I asked him once why he didn't wait for his workers to take care of those details.

"Well, Mr. Kelly, I do it because it enhances service. I don't want people waiting any longer than necessary. I don't mind. I enjoy people."

He wouldn't stop calling me mister. I called him Nate and he called me Mister Kelly. I asked him not to, but he said he always called his passengers mister and madam, no matter what their ages, and couldn't stop now.

He also made public address announcements on the train. That's how most people knew him. He had a sincere voice. I wish you could have heard him. You'd know what I mean.

A while ago I wrote about Nate Brawner and said he was about ready to retire. People sent me letters and cards addressed to Nate and asked me to pass their congratulations along to him. Those people said they had ridden with Nate and wanted to thank him for his years of service. A couple people even sent gifts.

I gave the stuff to Nate on his last trip. He cried some. He said he couldn't help it. He said he had no idea people felt that way about him. He said he had no idea passengers even knew he was alive.

That was last month. He had just turned 65, although he looked years younger.

While Kenny Brawner was introducing himself on the telephone, I was thinking that his voice sounded just like Nate's and was about to tell him so. I didn't get the chance.

"I'm sorry to have to tell you this," he said, and I knew what was coming. "Nate passed away today."

He said his brother suffered a heart attack Monday while bowling.

Nate loved bowling. He told me he was going to do a lot of bowling in his retirement years. He was going to take his wife on a trip, and he was going to--well, he was going to do many of the things that a person who comes up the hard way never gets the chance to do.

"They took him to one hospital," Kenny Brawner said, "and worked on him and they took him to another hospital by helicopter. They worked on him all night, but they couldn't save him."

I told Kenny Brawner how bad I felt. He thanked me. Kenny is just as polite as Nate. It must run in the family.

I'm going to fly west in March for a vacation and I will change planes in Chicago. Nate was going to meet me at the airport. We were going to get together. We had it planned.

He was going to bring his wife. Her name is Jewel. We've never met, but judging by the way Nate talked about Jewel, she was.

One final thought. I've interviewed my share of famous and powerful people. Most of them could have learned plenty from Nate Brawner -- make that Mister Nate Brawner.

So Long, Nate, and Thanks For Those Memories

Chicago, IL -- Billie Barrett, of the gospel-singing Barrett Sisters, turned off 111th Street and onto the Dan Ryan Expressway, a busy highway that cuts through some of the best and worst of Chicago.

Nobody in the car was exactly sure who Dan Ryan was or what he did to get such an important highway named after him.

"He was some sort of politician," said the tall slender man everybody calls J.W. He had come in from California to attend the service.

We had just come from burying Nate Brawner at Holy Sepulchre Cemetery, which is near several other cemeteries on the outskirts of Chicago. Now Billie, J.W. and Dolores, who is another member of the Barrett Sisters, were taking me to the train.

The Lake Shore Limited would take me home. The Lake Shore was Nate Brawner's train, a fact not lost on any of us.

"He did love those trains so," said Billie.

Nate worked on trains for 43 years. He worked his way up from shining passenger's shoes to chief of passenger services.

His job was to make people on the Lake Shore comfortable and happy. He did his job well.

He was smart, polite and had enough stories to make a long train trip seem short.

Nate retired about a month ago. He died of a heart attack a couple days ago.

He hadn't even cashed his first retirement check. The special plaque Amtrak got for him hadn't even been presented. When they talk about life not being fair, they are talking about things like that.

There was quite a send-off for Nate. They had it at A.A. Rayner and Sons, a funeral parlor on E. 71st Street.

"I've been here many times," said the man who stood next to me at the wake, "and I've never seen such a crowd."

The seats in the large room were taken long before the service started. People were standing in back and along the walls. More were waiting in line to get in.

"It's a tribute to Nate," said the man next to me.

The funeral parlor was warm. People read their programs and then used them as fans.

There were lots of people and lots of grief. Nate's wife, Jewel, was the strongest of all. She stood straight and gave each mourner a smile and a hug and a few words to make them feel better. I could see why Nate looked forward to coming home from his trips.

Life hasn't been easy for Jewel. Her first husband passed on at a young age. Her son Keith drowned not long ago. And now Nate.

According to the program, Nate's real name was Napoleon, although I've never heard anybody call him that. The program also said he was in the Army during World War II, bowled in three leagues, was a member of the South Eberhart Street Improvement Club, and the Duces, a social club.

Listed in the program were Nate's three daughters, one son, three stepsons, four brothers and 14 grandchildren. One of the daughters, Patty, wrote something and had it read during the service.

"My daddy was my refuge and strength," is part of what Patty wrote.

The service started with a prayer. Then the Barrett Sisters sang gospel. Billie Barrett and her husband and Jewel and Nate were close.

John Williams, a member of the Duces, spoke. He didn't talk long, but he hit home.

"All of us who knew him loved him. He brought us so much happiness. When you saw him, he smiled. He didn't frown. He always looked for the good side in everybody."

The Barrett Sisters came back for another song. Then the Rev. Robert Lowery delivered the eulogy.

"It isn't the quantity of life," he said, "it's the quality of life."

"Amen," said the mourners.

"If you want to keep this brother alive," said Lowery, "then reflect on him from time to time and remember the good he did in his life."

They ended the service with "When the Saints Go Marching In" and "My Buddy."

On the way to the cemetery, in a procession that stretched seven blocks, Billie talked about how Nate enjoyed jazz and gospel music.

"He even liked to sing a little," Billie said, "and he was an excellent dancer."

The Brawners and the Barretts attended many social events together. Billie said that whenever Nate saw a lady without an escort he would ask her for a dance.

"He didn't want anybody left out or feeling bad."

When Billie dropped me at the train station, she told me to have a pleasant trip. I refrained from saying that would be easy if only Nate was still taking care of the Lake Shore Limited's passengers.

People Like Nate Brawner Aren't Easily Forgotten

The caller identified himself as Gary McKenzie, an official with Amtrak. He said he worked in the company's Washington, D.C., headquarters.

"I understand you wrote some articles about an Amtrak employee named Nate Brawner," McKenzie said in a polite way. "Do you remember him?"

I was tempted to say that if Amtrak had more employees like Nate Brawner, more people would ride trains.

Instead, I said, "Yes, I remember. You don't forget people like Nate Brawner."

McKenzie explained that Amtrak has an annual contest to reward employees for outstanding service. Awards are presented in six categories, including Amtrak Employee of the Year.

"Nate Brawner has been nominated," McKenzie said.

I said I was glad somebody had the good sense to do so.

McKenzie said Amtrak had 22,000 employees, 339 had been nominated and a dozen or so would get awards. The selections will be made by 10 Amtrak officials, who are members of something called the President's Award Committee, McKenzie said.

"The competition is stiff."

I don't know how the committee makes its selections, but I know something about one of the people they are considering.

Nate started on the railroad shining passenger's shoes. It took a lifetime, but Nate worked himself up to chief of passenger services on Amtrak's Lake Shore Limited, which connects Chicago and New York.

It takes the Lake Shore five hours or so to get from Utica to New York City. I've make the trip many times. When Nate was on the train, the ride seemed shorter.

Nate retired last October. I had the honor of riding with him on part of his last trip. He said he was looking forward to retirement. I'm not so sure. He had tears in his eyes while telling me he was going to be happy.

I would not have been surprised if Nate had changed his mind at the last minute and kept on working, but he didn't. He died one month later. Heart attack.

At the wake, which was in A.A. Rayner and Sons Funeral Parlor, E. 71st Street, Chicago, I noticed that Nate's wife, Jewel, made sure he was wearing his Amtrak lapel pin. Nate's job meant a great deal to him.

On the way to the cemetery that day, Nate's friend Billie Barrett, of the gospel-singing Barrett Sisters, remarked that Nate was always pointing out Amtrak's good points to anybody who would listen.

"Amtrak, Amtrak, Amtrak," Billie said, "He was always talking about Amtrak. He did love those trains so."

I'd love to sit Billie down with that Amtrak selection committee.

McKenzie said the committee was looking for information about the nominees.

"We're interested in any information we can get."

I told McKenzie I would send my thoughts to the committee, and added that nothing I could put in writing would do Nate justice.

Amtrak will present its awards at the end of March, McKenzie said. He promised to call and tell me the results.

I'm keeping my fingers crossed. It will be a shame if Nate doesn't win something.

Nate Brawner's Policy Earns Amtrak Award

The New York City bound Lake Shore Limited was running along the east bank of the Hudson River, if I remember correctly, on the day I asked Nate Brawner about his lapel pin.

"Well, sir, this is a service excellence pin," Nate said. He took it off and handed it to me for closer examination. "I was awarded it three months ago."

Nate, who was two months shy of 65 at the time, said he was proud to have been given such an honor by Amtrak, his employer.

Nate said it wasn't Amtrak's highest employee award, but that it was special to him because his selection was based on a letter a pleased passenger had written to the company.

And the award had come just in time, Nate said. His Amtrak career was just about finished and there wasn't time to be considered for any other awards.

He had worked on railroads for 43 years, starting out as a bus boy and ending up on the Lake Shore Limited as chief of passenger service, a fancy way of saying it was his job to make sure folks got fed and made comfortable.

Nate retired last October. He died in November. Heart attack.

In the lapel of the suit they buried him in was the Amtrak service pin that made him so proud. Jewel, his wife, made sure he had it on.

Nate was not an Amtrak VIP. He didn't make policy, but he knew how to take care of passengers. He told me something once that applies to more than just the people working for Amtrak. I was smart enough to write it down.

"I've never considered what I do to be menial work. It's important work. The passengers are buying a service and they've got a right to expect good service. If you don't give the service in the right tone and with the right attitude, you're defeating the whole purpose of your job."

Nate was right about that, but he was wrong about something else. He said it was too late in his career to be considered for another employee award.

Two months ago, Nate was nominated for Amtrak's Distinguished Service Award. Only the Employee of the Year award, which goes to an active Amtrak employee, ranks higher.

The competition for the Distinguished Service Award is keen. Amtrak presents only one or two a year. Just to be nominated is an honor.

A committee of Amtrak officials vote on the awards and not before the nominee's record is researched. I know this because I was questioned by an Amtrak person last month who wanted to know about Nate.

I telephoned the Amtrak person yesterday. He said that before submitting his findings to the selection committee, he had talked to Nate's minister, neighbors and others.

"Did you know Mr. Brawner raised money every year to fight sickle-cell anemia?"

I said I hadn't been aware of that, but wasn't surprised.

The Amtrak person said he checked with the railroads Nate worked for before joining Amtrak.

"We couldn't find one complaint. What he did in the way of passenger service over all those years, epitomizes everything we want to see in all of our employees."

One of the things taken into consideration by Amtrak's selection committee were letters sent by people from the Utica area, passengers who had ridden with Nate and knew he had been nominated for an award. Two of those letters, the Amtrak person said, were read out loud at a meeting of the selection committee.

Nate Brawner has won Amtrak's Distinguished Service Award.

Nate's wife hasn't yet been told about the award. Amtrak will soon contact Jewel, who lives in Chicago, and invite her to Washington, D.C. for a dinner. Nate's award will be presented to her at a ceremony the following day. Congressmen, Amtrak officials and other VIPs will be there.

"This is quite a big deal," the Amtrak person said.

I can see it now. Jewel Brawner will step up to the podium and smile, determined not to cry. With grace, charm and dignity, she will thank Amtrak and say how proud she is to accept the award, which is just how Nate would have handled himself.

Dear Amtrak: So Far, So Good

Dear Amtrak,

I'm here in Detroit. Thanks for asking my opinion about your service. I found your questionnaire waiting on my bed when I boarded the Lake Shore Limited in Utica at the beginning of this trip.

By the way, I made good use of the snacks and wine you put in my room.

I was expecting the refreshments, but not the package of stationery, pen and post cards. Thank you. I'll make good use of those things.

You ought to make more gestures of that sort. It lets passengers know you are interested in their business, something they haven't always been sure about.

As for the questionnaire, do many people fill them out? Probably not.

If you really are interested in what passengers have to say, I'll let you know.

That will have to wait, though. It's too soon to give you an honest opinion, although I must admit that things have gotten off to a good start.

The Lake Shore was about 30 minutes late when she arrived in Utica, but the time was made up during the night, and we got to Toledo almost on schedule.

This morning's breakfast in the dining car was excellent. The fresh flowers are a nice touch.

I must tell you, though, that the people at my table were grumpy. I wish I had been seated at the table across the aisle. They seemed to be having a nice conversation over there.

That's the thing about eating in the dining car. Sometimes you are seated next to interesting and enjoyable people, and sometimes you get what I got this morning.

I'm not blaming you, Amtrak. I realize there isn't anything you can do about grumpy passengers. Maybe they were out of sorts because they didn't sleep well. I slept great; always do on your trains.

I got off the Lake Cities, which runs between Toledo and Detroit, earlier today. Things went fine on that train, too.

By the way, Detroit's train station doesn't deserve to be called a train station. It's more like a tin garage.

My cab driver showed me the old station. Now that's a train station -- massive and imposing. I'll bet the inside is impressive, too, unless it has been allowed to deteriorate.

The driver said it hasn't been used for a long time. It's a shame to see buildings such as that not being used.

Utica's train station, on the other hand, is being used. People in Detroit would be jealous if they could see it.

Back to the purpose of this letter. You are doing OK so far, Amtrak, but I'll be going several thousand more miles with you on this trip, and I think it best that I wait until it's over before giving you my opinion on how the country's railroad is being run.

But I will share a couple observations with you now.

The public address systems on your trains leaves something to be desired. You ought to do something. It doesn't do much good to have conductors make announcements if we can't understand them.

While I'm on the subject, the P.A. systems in many of your terminals are no bargain, either.

I'll tell you something else. The trains are too warm. You could save energy and make everybody more comfortable by lowering the thermostat.

By the way, the view from the train today was interesting. It would have been nicer if there wasn't so much garbage along the tracks. It looks like people are using Amtrak's right of way as a dump.

I have to close now. I'm on my way to a place north of Detroit called Utica. That's right, Utica, just like the name of the place I come from.

I'm going to rent a car here, ride there and take a quick look around. Then it's back to Detroit and onto your train No. 351, the Wolverine, for the ride to Chicago.

Expect another letter from me soon. I'll let you know how you're doing.

All the best,
Joe Kelly

Utica's Best - Even in Michigan

Utica, MI -- Within minutes after arriving here, I was able to confirm that this Utica got its name from the Utica in New York.

The evidence is in old newspapers at the Utica Public Library on Auburn Avenue, a library much smaller than the Utica Public Library on Genesee Street.

I learned that this place was called Harlow, after a town in England, until 1833, "when immigrants from Utica, NY wanted to call it Utica."

There was a big squabble about the name change, but the Utica New Yorkers were in the majority and got their way when the name was put up for a vote.

The person who suggested the name change was one Gurden Leech, who built the first hotel here and helped publish the Utica Citizen newspaper.

People living here now are thankful Mr. Leech came along. Besides being named Harlow for awhile, this place was once called Hog Hollow. Utica is a much better name.

Utica Public Library is next door to Utica City Hall, which shares a modern building with the Utica Police Department.

I took a walk around Utica, which has a Clinton River going through town, and is just down the road from Rochester and Troy.

I saw the Utica Bakery, Utica Florist, Utica Prime Meat Shoppe, Utica Health Spa, Utica Amusement Park, Utica Collision, Utica Prescription Center, Utica Steel, West Utica Elementary School, Utica Fuel Oil, Utica Novelty Co. and went into the Utica Barber Shop, owned and operated by Carl Zawadzki.

"This is a nice place, nice people," Zawadzki said as he clipped the hair of Walter Rynrak, 79.

"There's a lot of building going on," Zawadzki said. "Things are popping up all over town."

Walter nodded in agreement. He said people and businesses were moving here to get away from crime in Detroit.

Utica, at the crossroads of Michigan routes 59 and 53, is 20 miles north of downtown Detroit, one of several bedroom communities around here.

"Crime is something we don't have to worry about," Zawadzki said. "Very quiet here. No problems."

He said Utica's police department has three cars and four officers. The fire department is volunteer. There is one ambulance.

They raided a house for drugs a few months back," said Harry Randall, who was waiting for his turn in Carl's chair. "Drugs are a problem everywhere these days."

I inquired as to Utica's weather.

"Last three winters were mild," Zawadzki said, "got hardly any snow."

"We got a total of three inches," Rynrak said, "and it was gone in no time."

On the barber shop's wall is a picture of Zawadzki in Korea. He was in an artillery unit. The picture shows him cutting hair.

Any problems facing Utica?

"We've got a woman mayor," Zawadzki said. "The first one ever. She's doing an excellent job. She just got elected last fall."

Must be some problems, I said.

Traffic was the only thing Zawadzki could come up with. There's too much.

"The roads can't handle it. They are going to widen the roads."

There's a new motel in town, which is where I went for the night. Kids were there from Utica High School, all dressed up, celebrating.

"Prom night," said the desk clerk, as she asked for a credit card and driver's license.

She saw my address and laughed. "Can't get away from Utica, can you?"

"Can't say as I want to," I said.

"You know something," she said, "neither do I."

Joe Kelly

Signs on the Road

While traveling in Vermont, I spotted a sign outside a tavern near Killington, a popular place to ski.

"Stop In For A Cold BrewSKI."

I was in Denver when I spotted this sign outside a used car lot: "If life gives you a lemon, trade it in."

And while riding the California Zephyr, I saw a tire repair shop on the outskirts of Sparks, Nevada. There was a billboard with large letters and this message: "The World's Best Place To Take A Leak."

These are signs I'm still waiting to see:

Outside a dry cleaner:	Lawsuits cleaned and pressed.
Outside a classroom:	Math teachers know all the angles.
Outside a flower shop:	Florists are petal pushers.
Outside an all-female law office:	Women lawyers make better motions.
Outside an elevator repair company:	We have our ups and downs.

Outside a barn:	Crime doesn't pay and neither does farming.
Outside a church:	If you must talk during the service, let it be a prayer.
Outside a cemetery gate:	Inter here.
Outside a gas and electric company:	Power to the people.
Outside a tavern:	Draft beer, not people.
Outside a billiard hall:	Shoot pool, not people.
Outside a barbershop:	Hair conditioned.
Outside a coroner's office:	Autopsy is a dying profession.
Outside a psychiatrist's office:	You're never alone if you have schizophrenia.
Outside a mayor's office:	Be sincere -- Even if you have to fake it.
Outside a beauty salon in the Bronx:	Yankee Clipper.

More Than One Person Has Love Affair With a Train

Chicago, IL -- Tell somebody you are going across the country on a train and you'll get one of two reactions: shock or envy.

The shocked reaction comes from people who haven't fallen in love with trains, people who just want to get from one place to another as fast as possible.

The look of envy comes from people who, when possible, arrange their schedules to permit them to indulge in their love affair with trains.

I fall into the latter group, which is why I took the Lake Shore Limited to Chicago. The train left Utica almost on time.

I went directly to my sleeping compartment. Amtrak calls them roomettes.

Whatever, they are the perfect size for somebody traveling alone, assuming that the somebody is not the size of a professional football or basketball player. Actually, the smaller and shorter you are, the more you will enjoy the roomette.

Edgar Pinkney, the sleeping car porter, explained the light switches and air conditioning and pointed to a button marked "porter".

"Press that if there's anything you need during the night."

The roomette has a wide seat and a stool. There is a large window, a tiny toilet, a tiny closet, a water dispenser, a sink that folds out of the side wall and a surprisingly comfortable bed that pulls out of the back wall.

When pulled out, the bed occupies every inch of the room, thus making it impossible to fall out of bed during the night. Unfortunately, it also makes going to the bathroom rather difficult.

Some people have trouble sleeping on trains. I don't.

I watched the moon and relaxed with the Lake Shore's gentle motion. I was asleep before Rochester.

I was awake in Cleveland at 7:30 and by 8 I was in the dining car. I had bacon, eggs, toast and coffee. Breakfast is the best meal Amtrak serves.

The diner was busy. I watched the onboard service chief, which is the title Amtrak gives the person in charge of the dining car and all other passenger services on the train.

She was good. She stood in the back of the car and watched the waiters. When they fell behind, she served a table for them or cleaned away dishes.

I heard her scold a waiter because of the way he was carrying a tray. Later she gave him a smile.

She was so good she reminded me of the man who had the job before her, Nate Brawner. This woman didn't miss much. Neither did Nate.

Nate was a friend. He died less than two months after he retired. After his death, he was awarded one of the highest commendations Amtrak gives its employees. His family accepted in his behalf.

We pulled into Toledo nearly on time. Then came Elkhart, South Bend, Gary and Hammond -- all in Indiana.

Back in my room, I got talking about trains with Mr. Pickney. He has been on the railroad for 19 years, the past 11 on the Lake Shore.

"With the airplane you go up and you go down," he said. "What do you see on the airplane? On the train you see this beautiful country."

The train was slowing for Chicago. The onboard service chief made her public address system announcements. She did it the way Nate once did -- with feeling.

Mr. Pinkney wanted to help with my bag. I asked him how long he would keep working on trains.

"Just as long as they will let me," he said. "Just as long as they will let me."

In Chicago's Union Station I saw the Lake Shore's onboard service chief. She was hurrying across the terminal with her luggage. I caught up with her.

I introduced myself. She said her name was Mildred Askew.

I told her how much she reminded me of a gentleman named Nate Brawner. She said that pleased her.

"Nate Brawner trained me when I came to work for Amtrak," she said. "I hope to be as good as he was someday. With some more seasoning I think I can be."

I'll say this for the lady, she has set a high goal for herself.

Joe Kelly

Wild Bill Farrow and His Railroad Cuisine

I've sampled Wild Bill Farrow's cooking, I've listened to his stories and I've asked for seconds of both.

Wild Bill's workplaces for 40 years were cramped, difficult-to-work-in kitchens in railroad dining cars. The tight quarters did nothing to diminish the taste of Wild Bill's down-home cooking, however.

His contention: The amount of room in a kitchen or the number of fancy gadgets has absolutely nothing to do with the quality of food.

Wild Bill took great pride in his cooking. Anybody, he reasoned, can cook in a kitchen that stands still. Cooking in a kitchen that rocks and rolls takes a bit more talent.

He took his skill and his laughter and spread it across 48 states as he criss-crossed the country cooking for seven railroads.

"It takes five years before the railroad gets in your blood," Wild Bill told me once. "After that, you can't leave it."

You might be wanting to know how Wild Bill came by his nickname. It has to do with his taste in clothes.

Aboard his trains, Wild Bill dressed in a chef's traditional white uniform. Off duty, he dressed like a cowboy.

He had a liking for kids and would stand on the corner in his Chicago neighborhood after returning from a trip and hand out candy. Picture, if you can, a man dressed as a Mexican cowboy, complete with crossed bandoliers on his chest and toy six guns on his hips, standing on a Chicago street corner surrounded by kids. He is quite a sight.

The kids gave Wild Bill his name.

I once worked as a waiter and had the distinct honor of serving food prepared by Wild Bill to passengers riding the Lake Shore Limited, the Amtrak train connecting Chicago and New York. Wild Bill laughed and joked all the way.

When the passengers were fed and the rush was over, I remember asking Wild Bill if he was as happy as he seemed.

"Yes, my man, I am," he said. "I can't ask for no more. My mind still works and I can kick my heels. It's a happy life. I've got a lot to be thankful for and nothing to complain about. I love everybody."

Wild Bill retired a few years ago and announced he was going fishing. Railroad dining will never again be quite so good.

Wild Bill comes to mind whenever I see the train exhibit outside the Children's Museum, corner of Railroad and Main streets, across from Union Station. The exhibit contains an engine, caboose and dining car.

The dining car, number 8031, was built in 1937 for the Santa Fe Railroad and once was part of the famed Santa Fe Super Chief, the crack train running between Chicago and Los Angeles.

When the train exhibit was put up by members of The Utica and Mohawk Valley Chapter of the National Railway Historical Society, I telephoned Wild Bill at his home in Chicago, told him about it and suggested that he probably worked on a similar dining car.

"My man, I worked in that car," said Wild Bill. "If that car was on the Santa Fe, I worked in it because I worked in every dining car the Santa Fe had.

I asked Wild Bill if he was enjoying retirement.

"Well, it's a 50-50 thing. There's some good and some bad. It takes getting adjusted."

I told him it sounded like he missed railroading.

"Oh, but I do. I take rides on my pass."

I asked if he regretted opting for early retirement at age 62.

"I've regretted it many times, but I don't like to let that be known. I don't want to be complaining. I'm a travelin' man. I've got it in me."

Wild Bill, 65, was married once. There were a couple kids. Maybe the traveling contributed to the breakup. I don't know.

He lives alone, but don't be sad for him because he isn't unhappy.

"I can still run, jump, kick my heels and dance. I thank the Lord for that. I live each day as if it were my last day and try to do something good for somebody."

I asked Wild Bill Farrow to visit Utica one day and sit in that old Santa Fe dining car and tell railroad stories. One day, maybe he will.

Nothing Like Riding the Train

Aboard the Lake Shore Limited -- Most of the train is asleep. It's nearing midnight. We are westerly bound, a half hour from home.

When we left Grand Central Station, four-and-a-half hours ago, the overhead lights were bright and passengers were talking about their weekends in New York. Many boarded with overnight cases and department store shopping bags.

Pulled by a red, white and blue Amtrak engine, we headed north through the night along the Hudson River, past Croton-Harmon, Poughkeepsie, Rhinecliff, Hudson and Albany, where we crossed the river and headed west along the Mohawk River and Barge Canal.

I've taken this trip many times. I can't think of a time when I haven't enjoyed the ride. Anybody who loves trains would.

By Schenectady, the loud talk had been reduced to whispers and the overhead lights had been dimmed. A few reading lights were on.

It is black outside. I can see myself in the window glass. Night trains are good places for reading and thinking.

If the Lake Shore is on time, it covers the 238 miles between New York and Utica in five hours and three minutes. The conductor just walked by, legs spread slightly, the way people do on moving trains. He said we were on time.

From Utica, the Lake Shore has another 722 miles until she reaches Chicago and turns around for the return trip.

The college student across the aisle, a young lady returning to Syracuse University, had been listening to her Walkman, volume so loud I could hear Lionel Richie. Now her earphones are off, her mouth is open and her eyes are shut.

Behind me is quiet, too. The couple has stopped talking about ballet.

That's another thing about the train. It isn't the best place for private conversations. I hadn't intended listening to them. There wasn't a choice.

On the trip down to New York, when it was light, the conductor pointed out places of interest.

We zipped through Ossining and past one of the guard towers at Sing Sing. A guard stepped out of his tower, rested a foot on the railing and looked down at the train. On the top of the fence was razor ribbon.

Down river from there we passed the United States Military Academy at West Point. The buildings are up on the hill. The river narrows at West Point. During the Revolution, a chain was placed across the river to keep the British out.

The Lake Shore has two sleeping cars, several coach cars, dining car, freight car and lounge car, where beer and mixed drinks are sold, making it the train's most popular car.

It's also the only place where smoking is allowed. Some people spend the entire trip in the lounge car.

Traveling is a good way to meet people and it's easiest on trains. If there isn't anyone interesting in the next seat, you can go to the lounge car, if you can stand the smoke.

I once met a young man on the Lake Shore. He worked for Kodak. He stood on the platform at Croton-Harmon and hugged a young woman good-bye. They hugged for a long time. They looked good together.

The young man boarded the train and took the seat next to mine. As the train started up, the young woman walked along next to our window and smiled at him and waved until the train picked up speed.

"We're engaged," he said.

I remember him saying that his girlfriend had a job in New York City. He had a good job in Rochester. Neither wanted to move. They were trying to figure out what to do.

People you meet on the road tend to talk about personal things. The problem is you never see them again to find out how things turned out.

Five hours and a couple of minutes after leaving New York City the Lake Shore Limited is pulling into Utica. A dozen of us got off. A conductor helped us out.

"Hope you had a good trip," the conductor said to me at the door.

"Thank you, sir," I said. "I always do."

Billy Butler: Engineer

Aboard the Empire State Express -- The eastbound six-car Amtrak train took the last curve before Utica and Billy Butler, who sat on the right side of the engine, looked at his watch and couldn't help but smile to himself. The Empire State Express was exactly on time.

Keeping his train on schedule has always been important to Butler, but never more so than this day, this important day.

Butler, 62, is an engineer. He is Amtrak's best engineer. Just ask me. I'll tell you. I've ridden with him.

Butler has worked on the railroad for 45 years. He has done his job with skill and unfailing good humor.

He started at age 17 in the New York Central baggage room and worked himself up. He shoveled coal when steam moved the engines which moved the country. Then he became an engineer, first on freights, later on passenger trains. He knows all there is to know about railroading.

Then, almost before he knew it, his career was over. This was his last run.

Earlier in the day, Butler drove from his home in New Hartford to Syracuse, as he has done for years, and climbed aboard the Empire State Express, relieving the engineer who had brought her in from the west.

And now Butler gently stopped the train on track number two, Utica. On a normal run, Butler would have stayed in the engine, looking at the sideview mirror, watching passengers board, waiting for conductor Tommy Van Duren to give the signal to highball. But this wasn't a normal run.

In the second floor windows of Union Station, Amtrak office workers waved goodbye to Butler. One employee, the woman who handles crew schedules, came out to the platform. Butler came down from the engine for a kiss and a hug. And there were hands to shake.

Butler has looked down from his engine for many years as people said goodbye on station platforms. Now it was his turn.

The goodbyes put Butler a minute or two, behind schedule.

"Don't worry," Butler said as he climbed back up into his engine, "we'll make it up."

Butler, dressed in an open necked shirt, maroon sweater, dark slacks and blue baseball cap, nudged the train forward and it slowly picked up speed. Railroad workers out in the yard stopped what they were doing and waved. Butler gave them a blast on the horn. Somebody called on the radio and wished him well.

"Have a good last run, Bill," said the radio voice. "And congratulations."

"I appreciate that," Butler said into the radio. "I really do."

It was the same all down the track. Engineers passing in the opposite direction called him on the radio.

"Good luck, Billy," one of them said.

Butler's train was in a section of track where the speed limit is 80 mph. He hit that speed and held it. When the limit increased, so did the train's speed. In an area where the speed limit is 110, the red digital numbers on the control panel in front of Butler read 109. The Mohawk Valley flashed by.

"You know," said Butler as he gazed at the Barge Canal, "I'm happy that I've gotten to this point, but I'm sad to be leaving."

It was then that they started coming forward out of one of the coach cars. There were five of them, all retired engineers, all living in the Utica area. They had grown up on the railroad with Butler.

The five of them got on in Utica. The idea was to provide an escort for Butler on his last run. They came into the engine one by one.

Joe Foley came up first. In the old days, Butler shoveled coal for Foley. That's when the two of them pulled freight trains across the state. Later, Foley was an engineer on the Empire State Express.

"He's the guy who taught the rest of us how to operate the turbo trains," Butler said.

Then came Tom Henry, Harold Longo, Bob Sanderl and Ted Spazanni.

And Tommy Van Duren, Butler's conductor for countless trips, came forward and gave his friend a pat on the back. Also along for the last trip was Virginia, Butler's wife.

In Albany, Butler and his entourage left the train. Another engineer would take her into New York. Butler and the others had lunch at the station, which was filled with people wanting to say goodbye to Amtrak's best engineer.

"It makes you feel good," he said.

Someone brought out a cake, decorated with Amtrak's logo.

Someone else pulled out a newspaper and passed it around. The front page picture showed what can happen when a driver tries to beat a train through a crossing. Three people were killed.

Twice in his career, Butler has come around a curve to find a car sitting across the tracks. Twice he felt a sick feeling in his stomach because he knew there was no way to stop in time. Both times, thank God, the cars had been abandoned. And then there was the winter when a car slid through a crossing and hit his train in the side.

"No one was hurt in any of them," Butler said.

It was time for Butler and his crew to relieve the crew of the westbound train which was pulling into the station. On the trip west, Butler and his friends reminisced about the railroad.

"Remember the time when..."

"There was the engineer who..."

"I'll never forget when..."

Back in Utica, railroad officials waited on the platform to congratulate Butler and somebody wanted to take his picture.

"Thanks," he yelled down from the engine, "thanks a lot."

A short time later, Butler pulled into Syracuse and checked his watch again. Beautiful. Eastbound and west, both runs were exactly on time. He had hoped it would end that way.

He cleaned out his locker, stopped at the bowling alley near the station for a couple drinks with his crew and went home. Billy Butler had a hard time believing it was over.

Last Stop, Pasadena - And It's Like Home

Pasadena, CA - This is incredible. The more I think about it, the more incredible it seems.

I am at the ninth annual reunion of former Utica-area people. They call themselves Uticans Unite of Southern California.

There are upwards of 400 people from all over California here at this city park, and most of them are wearing Utica T-shirts, hats and pins.

And all of them are talking about Utica. They grew up in the same area, but many of them are meeting each other for the first time here.

An overheard conversation: "Hi, my name is Lynn. Where in Utica are you from?"

"Hi, Lynn. I'm John. East Utica. How about you?"

"West Utica. You go to Proctor?"

And in seconds they are talking about Utica Free Academy-Proctor football games, Kewpee's, Utica theaters, the Uptown Grill and the Boston Store.

"Everybody here has a different memory of Utica," said Walter Renzi, UFA, Class of 1954. "I remember when they had the bandshell concerts on the Parkway. Those were good times."

Renzi said he grew up in Cornhill, moved to California 25 years ago and is a probation officer for Los Angeles County. He has attended all the Utica parties except the first one.

Tim Pasik, Notre Dame High School, Class of 1977, is a newcomer to California. I asked why he moved away from Utica.

"I don't like to think of it as moving away. Most of us were pulled away because of the job situation. The weather played a part, too.

"These Uticans here love to celebrate their roots," he said. "That's why I love coming here and being around them."

Pasik said one of his best memories was the Boilermaker Road Race, which he has run the past four years.

I said I could get him an application for the next Boilermaker.

"That's okay," he said. "I've already entered."

From where I am writing this, I can hear people at the party playing Utica trivia. The rules are simple. Somebody asks a question about Utica and people jump in with the answers.

The softball tournament has ended. East and west Utica beat north and south Utica. When it gets darker, they will show slides and a videotape of Utica.

I can see two Matt's beer balls, and many people here are wearing Matt's T-shirts, hats and aprons.

By the way, before lunch was served, a blessing was given by a priest -- a Utica priest, of course -- Father Ignatius Militello, who now lives in Sun Valley. He celebrated his first mass in Utica's Saint Mary of Mount Carmel Church on May 25, 1952.

I've been here several hours now and haven't heard one negative comment about Utica.

Two people who talked bad about Utica showed up at the first Utica party. They weren't asked back.

"We don't allow people to talk down on Utica here," said Steve Burchesky, a party organizer. He has lived here for 15 years and owns a company that produces industrial safety films.

"I think of Utica a lot. I'm real fond of Utica. The reason I'm out here is because of my job."

Jobs are the reason most people here give for leaving Utica.

Joanne Seaken Haren had a long-time dream of working for a major league baseball team. She applied to the Dodgers and got one.

"I came to California for the opportunity," she said. "I couldn't work for a major league team in Utica. I come to this party to rejoice in my memories of Utica, to celebrate my hometown."

I got talking to Al DiRoberto, UFA, Class of 1970. His Utica Devils T-shirt caught my eye. I asked why so many people showed up at the party every year.

"There isn't the sense of community out here like there is in Utica. We have big walls in our backyards. Out here you live in a neighborhood of strangers. People come to the party to get that sense of community back--for one day a year."

But not everybody at the party is a former Utican. There is at least one part-time Utican, Jim Burton, UFA, Class of 1949, who spends part of the year managing the company he owns here and the rest of the time in Utica.

"I have to go back home to get my sanity," Burton said. "I get sick of the crowds here. There are good things about Southern California and bad things. The same is true of Utica."

And there is at least one current Utican at the party. Her name is Dawn Vatalaro, Proctor, Class of 1979, now a travel agent with AAA.

She flew in from Utica last night for the party and will fly out tomorrow. This is her third Utica party.

"It's great being here. You can feel the pride everybody has in Utica."

I have to wrap this up now, but not before pointing out two things I've learned.

One, these people at the party love Utica, always will. Some of them are homesick.

Two, you don't appreciate something the way you should until you don't have it anymore.

Traveling to Ohio For a Kewpee's Hamburger

Aboard the Lake Shore Limited -- Last night, while sitting in Utica's Union Station waiting for the westbound Lake Shore Limited to take me to Toledo, Ohio, I was thinking about Kewpee's.

I had my fingers crossed. I worried whether the train would get me to Toledo in time to catch the bus to Lima, Ohio. Lima is home to Kewpee's -- three Kewpee's.

Which is why I was going to Lima. I have not had the pleasure of eating a Kewpee's hamburger for 17 years. Seventeen years!

Kewpee's started doing business in Utica on Oneida Square in 1938 and went out of business in 1973. A Burger King now occupies the site.

While waiting for the train last night, I remembered back to the 1950s and being taken to Kewpee's. The car hop would attach a tray of hamburgers, French fries and beverages to the car window, rolled halfway down.

I remembered the 1960s and cruising Genesee Street and stopping at Kewpee's.

A picture of the red neon sign in Kewpee's window flashed into my mind. The sign faced the parking lot and stated: "Please Do Not Blow Horn. Use Lights For Service."

My Kewpee's memories were interrupted last night by a public address announcement. The Lake Shore was arriving. It was 12:55 in the morning. The train was about 10 minutes behind schedule.

Within a couple minutes I was on the train and in my sleeping compartment. The train started with a lurch. I looked at my watch. A Kewpee's hamburger would be in my hands within 14 hours.

Going out of state for a hamburger might seem unusual to some, but not to people who frequented Kewpee's on Oneida Square.

Several people asked me to bring Kewpee's hamburgers back from this trip. I declined. My feeling was that no matter how good the hamburger was in Ohio, it wouldn't taste like much after being transported home to a microwave.

This morning I went into the Lake Shore's dining car. I was shown to a table occupied by a woman in her 30s. The opening conversation was the same as it always is when you meet someone while traveling.

"Where are you heading?" she asked.

I told her.

"Business or pleasure?"

I explained that I was going to Ohio for a hamburger.

Her eyebrows raised in surprise. She had never heard of Kewpee's. I gave her a three point crash course.

1. Kewpee's was once a chain, headquartered in Ohio. There are only six left, the three in Lima, two in Michigan and one in Wisconsin.

2. Uticans called it "Kewpee," "Kewpee's," or "the Kewpee." Whatever, it was an institution, a landmark, a treasure.

People went there day and night. The menu consisted of hamburgers, French fries and beverages.

3. What's a word that means better than delicious? That's the word I would use to describe Kewpee's hamburgers. Over the past 17 years, those hamburgers have gotten even better tasting in my mind.

Breakfast is over. I'm back in my sleeping compartment. My watch says six hours to Kewpee's.

I'm no longer worried about being late. At this rate, the train will get me to Toledo in time to catch the bus to Lima.

But I have a new worry. What if Kewpee's hamburgers don't taste as good as I remember?

Kewpee's Lives in Lima, Ohio

Lima, OH -- To get here, I have taken the overnight train, which pulled out of Utica after midnight and deposited me in Toledo, Ohio, at 9:36 this morning. From the train station it was a cab ride across town to the Greyhound Bus station. Then it was almost a two hour bus ride down I-75 to Lima.

This, however, is a small price to pay for being able to eat a Kewpee's hamburger, which is the reason for this trip.

I am in a van driven by Harry Shutt, who owns three of the last six remaining Kewpee's. In the backseat are Harry's wife, Myrna, and their son, Scott. They insisted on picking me up at the bus station.

We are listening to Harry, 58, who has worked for Kewpee's since the 1950s and who has owned Lima's three Kewpee's restaurants for 10 years.

Harry enjoys talking. And when the talk is of Kewpee's, to which Harry is devoted, the only time he stops talking is to take a deep breath.

"I'm told that at one time there were 400 Kewpee's around the country," Harry was saying. "If it's not the oldest franchised restaurant in the country, it's one of the oldest."

Kewpee's was a loosely organized, now defunct, national chain. Harry now owns the Kewpee's name and trademarks. There is still a Kewpee's in Racine, Wisconsin, Harry said, and two in Lansing, Michigan.

As we drove toward the downtown Kewpee's at Market and Elizabeth streets, Harry talked about the retail stores that have moved from downtown Lima, population 50,000, into the suburban shopping malls. Downtown is now mostly offices, banks, and government buildings.

Which made me think of Utica. In fact, looking out the van's window I was reminded of Utica.

"We have to fight tooth and nail to maintain our dollar volume," Harry said. "McDonald's is our major competitor. (They have five restaurants in Lima.) But everybody else is here, too."

The Kewpee's at the busy intersection of Allentown and Cable has the biggest competition. Within a block of that Kewpee's, various restaurant chains have opened up a total of 600 new seats within the past year, Harry said, but the Allentown Kewpee's remains number one in sales.

I asked Harry how he was able to successfully compete against the fast food giants.

"We're an old institution, we've maintained our image and we've kept our quality high."

And Kewpee's has Harry. He is community minded, serves on numerous committees and boards, and if Harry wasn't so good at making hamburgers, he would have had a brilliant career in marketing and promotions.

That has resulted in loyal customers in Lima, near Lima and far from Lima. When I telephoned Harry to tell him I would be coming to Lima for a hamburger, he sounded not at all surprised. It is not uncommon for people to travel here from long distances to get a Kewpee's hamburger, he said.

"We have loyal customers."

Harry's other Kewpee's is on Bellefontaine Street, in a building that once was a Robert Hall clothing store. Harry renovated it. The restaurant seats 180.

But it was the downtown Kewpee's that I was most interested in. It was built in 1938, the same year Utica's Kewpee's was built on Oneida Square.

Utica's Kewpee's was demolished in 1973 to make room for a Burger King. I asked Harry about that. He said the owner of Utica's Kewpee's, a Toledo man who once headed the Kewpee's chain, got an offer from Burger King he couldn't refuse.

We pulled up to Kewpee's. I tried not to look anxious. This was the moment I had been waiting for.

The first place I looked was above the front door. The large Kewpee doll was in place, just like it was in Utica. In fact, the building is almost the same as Utica's, except for one side, altered to accommodate a drive through window.

"Two years ago we added a drive through," Harry said. "Until then we had curb girls."

Harry said the drive through was more efficient and faster than curb service.

The drive through was busy. It was crowded inside, too, and it was long past the lunch hour.

With minor exceptions, the interior is just what I remember from Utica's Kewpee's.

We took seats in a booth. Harry went behind the counter to check on something, giving Myrna a chance to talk about Kewpee's.

"They ran a survey in the paper," she said, "and for two years in a row people voted our coffee the best in Lima."

"And our hamburgers won, too," Scott said.

Harry was back with a small menu, listing hamburgers, cheeseburgers, double burgers, with or without cheese, frosted malts and French fries.

He has added items that weren't on Utica's Kewpee's menu. Harry sells chili, yogurt, fresh baked pies, and has donuts, rolls and juice for breakfast.

I didn't need the menu. I've known for years what I would order if ever given the chance. It would be what I always ordered on Oneida Square.

"I'll have a hamburger with everything," I said, "a frosted malt and fries."

A Kewpee's hamburger with everything means you get it with catsup, mustard, onions and pickles.

The order was ready amazingly fast. The hamburger was wrapped in the same kind of wax paper I remembered. The Kewpee doll decorated the blue and white wrapper along with the saying, "Hamburg-pickle-on-top makes your heart go flippity-flop."

I unwrapped the hamburger. The patty was square, like I remembered. There was enough of it to stick out from under the roll.

While I ate, Harry talked about the importance of cleanliness, the importance of buying the right meat, the importance of grinding it fresh daily.

"You don't end up with quality unless you start out with quality," Harry said.

Scott asked, "Well, is it as good as you remember?"

I shook my head no, finished chewing and washed it down with frosted malt.

"It's better," I said. "It's better than what I remember."

Scott smiled.

Myrna said, "Thank you" in the way people do when your opinions are important to them.

As for Harry, he had an expression on his face that said any other answer from me would have surprised him.

Before leaving Lima, I stopped at Harry's other two Kewpee's for more hamburgers. I didn't want to, but I felt as if it was my, ahem, duty to do two more taste tests.

And one of these days, I'll get on the train and head over to Lansing and Racine to check out the Kewpee's there. Hey, somebody has to do these things.

Unscheduled Stop

Aboard the California Zephyr -- We had a close call about five minutes ago. The train almost hit a cement truck. A few passengers are still shaking.

They aren't shaking scared. They are shaking mad. We are stuck here at this railroad crossing for we don't know how long while they inspect the train to see if the emergency stop caused any damage.

It's 10:10 a.m. and the Zephyr should be speeding east. Instead, she is dead in her tracks.

We are in a wooded Utah valley east of Salt Lake City. As near as I can figure from the map on my lap, these are the Wasatch Mountains and the river off to the right is the Spanish Fork River, which is running muddy.

I can see a dirt road, but no houses. The leaves have turned red and orange. It reminds me of the Adirondacks.

An announcement is being made on the Zephyr's public address system. We are being told that the emergency stop caused flat spots on the wheels of one of our engines.

Amtrak inspectors are coming out from somewhere to check the engine before we are allowed to continue.

Let me explain how we came to be in this situation. The Desert Wind came up from Los Angeles. The Pioneer came down from Seattle. The Zephyr came across from Oakland.

The three trains met in Salt Lake City early this morning, became one and continued east as the California Zephyr.

The train is long and has three engines pulling us to Chicago.

The trip had been routine. That changed when the cement truck driver, someone with much daring and no brains, tried to get through the unguarded railroad crossing before we did.

The driver really was stupid. The Zephyr is fast and would have taken just seconds to get through the crossing. Utah isn't in such dire need of cement that the driver couldn't have waited a few seconds.

It is morning, thus eliminating the excuse that he was tired and in a hurry to get home after a long day.

The weather is beautiful, a few puffy clouds against blue sky, so visibility wasn't a factor.

Whatever the truck driver's reason, the Zephyr's engineer had to throw the engine into an emergency stop.

How close did we come to hitting the truck? I'm not sure. You can't tell from way back here in the sleeping car.

It must have been close, though. I've ridden more than a few trains and I can tell you that engineers don't make a habit of throwing their trains into an emergency stop.

It isn't good for the engine and it plays havoc on the people standing up in the club car with a drink in their hand.

I've just returned from a walk through the train. As far as I can tell, nobody has been hurt. Not even a bump on the head.

The only problems I heard about were from people who got their morning coffee dumped on them and an elderly lady who was standing in the aisle at the time and ended up sitting on the floor.

"Got knocked right on my ass," she said.

A conductor just walked by and said one of our engines will have to be taken from the train because of flat spots on its wheels. We will go to Chicago on two engines. He said we would be hours late.

I suggested to him that drinks in the lounge car should be on Amtrak. The people I said it in front of showed their agreement by applauding. The conductor was not amused.

Power is off on the train while they work on the engine. Toilets don't flush and air conditioning doesn't work when there is no power.

I still say drinks should be on the house.

The work took more than an hour. We've started rolling again, but the speed isn't what it should be. Our estimated arrival time in Chicago is between five and six hours late.

Anybody wanting to connect with another train in Chicago tonight can forget about that.

Things could have been worse, though, much worse.

Amtrak just announced that anyone forced to spend the night in Chicago because of a missed connection will get their hotel room, ground transportation and meals paid for.

Since my suggestions for free drinks were rejected, I'm going to buy one myself. There's someone driving this train with quick reflexes, and I want to drink to that engineer's good health.

In California With Schultz and Dooley

San Francisco, CA -- I have just spent 40 hours in San Francisco. I had great fun.

A couple hours were spent sleeping. The rest of the time was spent looking at the city. Hey, I can sleep anytime.

I decided to see all of San Francisco in less than two days. This is called being a tourist.

Since it was near dinner time when I arrived, my first intention was to get a before-dinner drink. But where?

I looked around until I found a bar that reminded me of Utica. The name of the bar is the Schultz and Dooley.

It's a small but comfortable bar on Kearny Street, between Sutter and Bush, in the Union Square district.

A couple sat at a table in the back. The bartender was pouring a beer for a woman wearing a San Francisco Giants baseball hat. The rest of the stools and tables were empty.

Situated in a place of prominence on the back bar were a pair of Schultz and Dooley mugs, made famous by all those years of Utica Club beer commercials.

The mugs were a welcome sight for someone far from Utica.

I told the bartender to pour me a cold Utica Club.

"Sorry, we don't serve that."

I asked for a Matt's.

"Sorry," he said, "we don't serve that either."

The bartender didn't even know what a Saranac was.

This was confusing. I was sitting in the Schultz and Dooley bar and couldn't get one of their beers.

I explained that I was from Schultz and Dooley's home.

"Another guy from Utica comes in here every Friday for lunch," the bartender said.

Poor guy is probably homesick, I figured.

I asked how the bar got its name.

"I'm not really sure, but it was because of those TV commercials they used to do. If you want to know more, you better talk to Mel, the owner."

I inquired as to when he would be in.

"Tomorrow, but Mel is a woman," the bartender said.

"Oh," I said.

My next stop was at an authentic Chinese restaurant in Chinatown called the Grand Palace on Grant Avenue. I ordered something I wasn't able to pronounce.

At the Grand Palace they play Willie Nelson songs on the jukebox, which is as strange as naming a bar the Schultz and Dooley and not serving Utica Club.

Being a tourist, I avoided cabs and took cable cars whenever possible.

"They seat 27 and hold 100," a veteran cable car rider told me, exaggerating only slightly.

He said there were three things to keep in mind when riding cable cars: There is always room for one more, hang on tight and if somebody rubs up against you as the car goes around a sharp turn it doesn't necessarily mean anything.

I rode the cable car to Fisherman's Wharf and took a cab over the Golden Gate Bridge. My driver, one of those up-beat kind of people, quickly pointed out that 11 people died during the bridge's construction and that 782 people have jumped off since then.

"Somebody jumps every month or so," he matter of factly said.

We then went to Lombard Street.

"It's the most crooked street in the United States," the cabbie said, "except for Wall Street."

Before leaving San Francisco, I stopped back at the Schultz and Dooley twice more. I wanted to ask Mel why she didn't serve any Utica beers.

Mel wasn't there either time, which means I'll have to go back there someday. I'm not complaining.

U.S.S. Oriskany: A Welcome Sight

Bremerton, WA -- The idea came to me while poking around David Ishii's bookstore on First Street in Pioneer Square, the historic section of Seattle.

Pioneer Square is where settlers came in 1852 to start what would become Seattle. Today, the square is filled with galleries, one-of-a-kind shops, restaurants, bars, entertainment and David Ishii's shop, where out-of-print and rare books are sold at reasonable prices and where each purchase is neatly wrapped in thick brown paper.

His store is two blocks from the waterfront and Puget Sound. Bremerton is on the other side of Puget Sound. Bremerton is where the U.S.S. Oriskany was put in mothballs.

The aircraft carrier is named after the Revolutionary War battle fought just up the road from Utica. Work on the Oriskany started too late for her to make it into World War II, but she saw action in Korea and Vietnam.

Standing there in David Ishii's shop, I knew what I had to do. I had to go see the U.S.S. Oriskany. I'd seen photographs of her and I'd seen her in "The Bridges of Toko-Ri," starring William Holden, but I wanted to see her for real. It would be a shame to be this close and not see her.

I walked four blocks to the ferry terminal, bought a $3.30 ticket to Bremerton, took the hour boat ride across Puget Sound and went directly from the dock to the gate of the Navy shipyard, officially called the U.S. Naval Inactive Ship Maintenance Facility.

After being refused entry by one guard, I was refused by his boss and worked my way up the chain of command until I was talking on the phone to a public affairs officer who was trying to enjoy a Saturday afternoon at home.

"If you'd come back on Monday I'd be happy to let you see the Oriskany," he kept repeating. I kept repeating that I had to catch a train on Sunday.

The officer was stubborn. I couldn't convince him to give up his day off and act as my escort. I never did get into the shipyard.

Which is not to say I didn't see the Oriskany.

My new friend Chuck, a driver for Bremerton's Arrow Cab Co., is an old Navy hand.

"Machinist mate on the (U.S.S.) Kitty Hawk," Chuck said after I settled into the backseat of his cab. "Served two tours in Vietnam."

I told Chuck about the Oriskany and explained the problem. He listened and then pulled away from the curb. Ten minutes later he stopped his cab in front of a row of mothballed ships, including aircraft carriers.

"That is the (U.S.S.) Hornet," Chuck said, pointing at the first carrier in the row, "and there's the Oriskany."

He was pointing to the carrier on the Hornet's left.

The only thing between us and the carriers was a chain-link fence and 50 yards.

The Oriskany, I must say, isn't much to see in her present state. Her gray paint looks good and I didn't see any rust, but she's closed up tight.

For the record, the Oriskany is 911 feet long, 225 feet tall and 197 feet wide. She once carried 80 aircraft and a crew of 3,200.

Last I knew, plans were to scrap the Oriskany. Folks in Oriskany, NY are hoping to get her anchor and display it in the village.

The Navy hasn't yet started taking the Oriskany apart, so if you ever get out here and have a hankering to see her, call the Arrow Cab Co. Ask for Chuck.

'Sir, Put on Clothes and Get Out of MY Room'

Seattle, WA -- Kitty corner from the Seattle Public Library, at Fifth Avenue and Spring Street, is the Kennedy Hotel.

The Kennedy is an older hotel and wasn't my first choice, but the Seahawks were at home and three conventions were in town, bringing to mind an old saying about beggars and choosers.

Don't get me wrong. They are friendly at the Kennedy.

"That will be room number 556, Mr. Kelly. We hope you enjoy your stay and if there's..."

I didn't catch the last part because I was already on the elevator pressing the "5" button. It had been a long day. I wanted to shower and flop into bed.

That was not to be. When I opened the door to 556 there was a man, whose ancestors come from somewhere in the Far East, in MY room and in MY bed.

He said something that sounded Japanese and probably meant, "There's only one bed in here and it's mine."

The man didn't seem too upset about me standing there, suitcase in hand, looking at him in MY bed. He even bowed, which isn't easy when you are sitting up in bed with no clothes on while trying to keep covered with a sheet.

Did I forget to mention he was naked in bed when I opened the door to MY room?

I tried to explain that he was in the wrong room by talking very slowly and pronouncing each word distinctly.

"Please--sir--put--on--your--clothes--and--get--out--of--MY--room."

This was said as I held out my room key and dangled it back and forth.

He responded by reaching over to the nightstand, picking up a room key and dangling it back and forth. If he hadn't been talking so fast, I might have been able to understand a few words.

I even tried sign language. I went through the motion umpires use when throwing a player out of the game. The fellow in MY bed must not have been a baseball fan because he didn't move.

Since I was the one with clothes on and since he wouldn't budge, I went to the front desk to get things straightened out.

"Call me picky," I said to the desk clerk, "but I only paid for a single, not a double."

The clerk discovered that he had given MY room to someone else and apologized, which I accepted because he gave me the key to room 336, the last vacant -- at least I hoped it was vacant -- room in this hotel and in all of Seattle.

A stranger in your bed is just one of the things you hate to have happen during a train trip. There are others.

For example, while riding the Empire Builder between Chicago and Seattle I wish I hadn't seen:

- Two conductors and assorted other Amtrak employees scratch their heads as they stood next to the train, which made an unscheduled stop in the middle of nowhere in North Dakota. They never did find the source of the smoke.

- A bumper sticker stating: "Don't let Seattle become another New York."

- The results of what can happen when the wrong button is pushed in Amtrak's combination toilet-shower. I learned the hard way that you flush the toilet by pushing the bottom button and that you activate the room's shower by pressing the top button. Or is it the other way around?

- A train attendant asking passengers if they had a tool capable of cutting through gold, as in a gold ring on a woman's finger. She slammed her finger in a door and it swelled up and needed to come off -- the ring, that is. Someone did have a tool and the ring was removed.

By the way, I should mention one more thing. I saw my Japanese friend once more after the brief encounter in MY room. It was in the coffee shop around the corner from the hotel.

Every seat in the place was taken. I think he was about to get off his stool, but then he saw me and stayed put.

He wasn't about to let me have HIS stool.

Vietnam Memorial: Impressive, Profound

Washington, D.C. -- "You can feel the sadness here, can't you?"

The question came from a young woman standing in the crowded walk in front of the Vietnam Veterans Memorial. The question wasn't directed at anyone and she got no answer.

But she was right. The sadness can be felt here. This town is filled with memorials, but none this recent.

I asked the young woman if she was here for a particular person. She said she was not.

"I just wanted to come and see it. It's so impressive in such a simple way, don't you think?"

Well put, I said.

On each end of the black granite wall of 58,132 names are directories, which makes finding a particular name possible. The names are inscribed on the wall in order of the date of death.

I ran my finger down a page in the directory until I came to Edward M. Brady, Utica. People didn't call him Edward, though. It was always Mark.

According to the directory, Mark was born June 23, 1947, and died July 6, 1967. His name can be found on panel 23E of the wall, line 17.

It took only a minute to find him. Some people touched names. One woman in her 40s kissed a name. I just stood and looked.

"Would you like a rubbing of a name?" asked a man wearing a blue sport coat and an identification tag saying his name was Robert Jackson, a volunteer with the National Park Service, which has charge of the wall.

Mark's name is high up on the wall. Jackson got a ladder and made the rubbing.

Jackson said he worked for the American Mining Congress, a trade association in Washington, during the week and did rubbings on weekends.

Jackson did two tours of duty in Vietnam.

I thanked him for volunteering to do the weekend work. The rubbings are a nice thing to take home.

"You're welcome," he said, "but this isn't work."

On the ground in front of the wall are items left by friends and relatives. There are many small U.S. flags, flowers and personal items, which on this day included photographs, medals, rings, letters, shoulder patches and a necklace.

Many are sealed in plastic bags for protection, like one containing a Purple Heart, dog tags, and baseball card collection.

The Park Service gathers items from the wall every so often and stores them in a Maryland warehouse. There is talk of one day using the items in an exhibit.

I didn't have anything of significance to place at the wall in honor of Mark, so I wrote a note. I wanted to make sure that something with Mark's name on it gets into that Maryland warehouse.

Even Tourists Dislike Tourists in Montana

I once rode Amtrak's Empire Builder from Chicago to Seattle, enjoying the scenery. Along the way I collected mostly useless information. This is only some of it:

- The "Empire Builder" was railroad tycoon James J. Hill's nickname.

- Niles, Illinois, has a replica of the Leaning Tower of Pisa, which can be seen as the train passes through town.

- Amtrak routes cover almost 24,000 miles of track.

- East of Minneapolis-St. Paul, the train skirts around Lake Pepin, which some people claim was the birthplace of water skiing.

- Rugby, North Dakota, which is between Minot and Grand Forks, is the geographic center of North America and there's a monument there marking the exact spot. The monument can't be seen from the train and the stop in Rugby isn't long enough to go looking. I did, however, have sense enough to step down from the train and walk around the station platform, thus enabling me to say that I once stood in the community which is in the center of the North American continent.

- The only states Amtrak doesn't run through are Maine, South Dakota, Oklahoma and Wyoming.

- Spuckie is another name for a submarine sandwich.

- Near the North Dakota-Montana border, passengers on the Empire Builder can see the remains of Fort Buford, where Chief Sitting Bull surrendered after the Battle of Little Big Horn.

- Message scribbled on the pay phone wall on the main street in East Glacier Park: "I don't like tourists."

- Message scribbled next to the message on the pay phone wall on the main street in East Glacier Park: "Even tourists don't like tourists."

- The Milk River, which can be seen from the train on the approach to Havre, Montana, was charted by Lewis and Clark. At certain times of the year, minerals are washed into the river giving it a milky look.

- Behind Havre's train station is a restored steam locomotive and tender, which, according to the sign, are 103 feet long, and weigh 764,680 pounds. The engine was put into service in 1930 and retired in 1955.

- The best place to get a beer and shoot pool in East Glacier Park is a place called the Park Bar. It is also the only place in East Glacier Park where those two things can be done.

The Man Who Made Alcatraz Pay Him Back

San Francisco, CA -- It is early afternoon. The boat crossing windy San Francisco Bay is filled with people wanting to tour the island of Alcatraz.

According to the guidebook in my hand, the following things are true:

- Alcatraz was named by Spanish explorers in 1769. They called it Isla de Alcatraces, which is Spanish for Island of Pelicans.

- Alcatraz was the site of the first lighthouse on the West Coast, 1854.

- Alcatraz was a U.S. Army fort from 1859 to 1933. During the Civil War it was the most heavily fortified site on the West Coast.

But that isn't the history that has drawn this boatload of tourists to Alcatraz. The island's 750,000 annual visitors are interested in something else.

From 1934 to 1963, the worst of the worst criminals went to Alcatraz. Al Capone, Machine Gun Kelly and Robert "Birdman"

Stroud were here. So were men whose names aren't as well known but whose crimes were as bad or worse.

At the Alcatraz dock, we get a map. We can tour the prison on our own or join a group and be escorted by a ranger from the National Park Service.

I go on my own and stop first in the museum, housing relics from the island's past.

In a hall outside the museum sits Leon "Whitey" Thompson, a living Alcatraz relic. Thompson was a prisoner on the island for four years. When Alcatraz was closed in 1963, Thompson was transferred to another prison.

Thompson, who has been out of jail and trouble since 1975, has written a book about himself and Alcatraz. He sells it here.

"Is it any good?" a woman from England demands to know.

Thompson is sitting at a table with an electric space heater behind him. The thick-walled buildings on Alcatraz are always damp and chilly.

"I think it's good," he says in a soft and deliberate voice, "but you'll have to judge for yourself."

The woman tells a friend to take a picture of her standing next to Thompson. She doesn't ask his permission.

"I've always wanted to be in a picture with a famous criminal," she says and laughs.

Thompson tries to laugh but doesn't quite succeed.

She does not buy Thompson's "The Last Train to Alcatraz," which sells for $13.95. Many others do.

The buyers ask Thompson questions as he autographs their books. I stand to the side, listening.

Thompson says he committed his first robbery at age 13 and later graduated to armed robbery. He says he never killed anyone.

"The book is true," he says. "I was a lot of bad things but I was never a liar."

When the tourists leave, we talk.

"Whitey" Thompson, so nicknamed because of his hair color, is 66 years old. Half his life has been spent in jail. Half.

"It took me a long time to grow up. I used to blame everybody but myself for my troubles. That's what people in prison do. They blame others."

When Thompson got out of prison in 1975, he got married.

"She turned my life around. She's the one who got me to write the book."

I asked about Alcatraz.

"I have nothing but total hate for this place, but I have to admit it's a beautiful island. I hate the island, but I love the island."

It really is a beautiful place, complete with flowers and a picture postcard view of San Francisco's skyline and the Golden Gate Bridge.

I asked Thompson what he did when not selling books.

He said he spent time in schools talking to young people, trying to keep them from making the mistakes he did.

I left the museum and toured the prison. It's smaller than I had imagined. But then the average number of prisoners was only 260.

Park ranger Marcus Combs was on duty in the cell house. I asked if he knew Thompson and which had been his cell.

Thompson's cell was in B Block, second level, third cell from the end. Although Combs said he wasn't certain, Al Capone might have also been in that cell at one point.

I asked Combs about Thompson. It is, after all, the National Park Service which gives Thompson permission to come out to Alcatraz on the day's first boat and sit in the museum with his books.

"You mean is he pulling our chain? I don't think so," Combs said. "I've gotten to know him and he is the most sincere person I've ever met."

The last boat of the day leaves Alcatraz at 4:35. I was on it. So was Thompson. We sat and talked.

I asked what it was like the first time he set foot on Alcatraz as a free man.

"When I went up to my old cell block, the sounds all came back to me. I was pretty emotional. Everyday here was survival."

Thompson left the boat carrying empty boxes. He said he would fill them with more books and return tomorrow.

"Alcatraz took a lot from me," he said, "but now it's providing me with a living."

Some 23,000 copies of the book have been sold. Today he sold 126, a little more than average.

Thompson said part of the money goes to the non-profit Golden Gate Park Association, of which Alcatraz is a part. The volunteer group is trying to improve the park system.

Thompson said he published the book himself, using money borrowed from everyone he knows, including police officers.

"And I've paid every cent back."

As Thompson, whose second book is due out this year, walked away, I was thinking he's probably the only ex-convict to make a buck out of Alcatraz.

But what a price he paid.

Some Travel Tips for Anyone Westward Bound

Several people have told me they are considering a trip west by rail, similar to one I once did.

Before buying their tickets, they may want to ask some questions about trains and about the west. In anticipation of their questions, here are the answers.

Q. Is it bad when you are out on the desert and the wind picks up and blows all that sand?

A. Not really. If you close your eyes, shut your mouth tight and hold your nose shut, it isn't bad at all.

Q. When traveling long distances through the desert by train, should you take care and not drink too many alcoholic beverages?

A. Sometimes too much isn't enough.

Q. Is it possible to describe what it's like driving on California freeways?

A. As a youngster, I once took my sled to the Parkway and did a belly whopper down the ski hill. I was totally out of control, hell bent for leather, scared to death, and only inches from death. But given the choice between 1000 belly whoppers and a short freeway drive, I'd take the ski hill every time.

Q. Did driving on the freeways teach you anything?

A. Yes. If I continue to do crazy things, one day I will hurt myself quite badly.

Q. Is the smog around Los Angeles as bad as people make it out to be?

A. Los Angeles? I never saw Los Angeles.

Q. Why should I take several days riding west on the train when an airplane will get me there in hours?

A. Ever hear of a train falling out of the sky?

Q. Trains can't be that much safer than airplanes, can they?

A. When was the last time a conductor asked you to fasten your seatbelt or gave you instructions for using the emergency oxygen?

Q. Were you frightened about being caught in an earthquake while in California?

A. Actually, I was hoping for an earthquake. I plan on retiring when I get all that money from the sale of my ocean front property in Phoenix, Arizona.

Q. Did you meet anybody interesting on the train?

A. Yes. A young couple on their honeymoon who had the sleeping compartment next to mine.

Q. Did you learn anything on the train?

A. Yes. Walls on the train aren't as thick as I thought.

Q. What did you enjoy most about being in a sleeping car?

A. Being next to a young newlywed couple on their honeymoon.

Q. Is it difficult falling asleep on the train?

A. Only if there's a young couple on their honeymoon in the next room.

Train's on Track, But What About Passengers?

Aboard the Empire Builder -- We've left Chicago and Milwaukee far behind. Minneapolis-St. Paul won't come until after midnight. I doubt I'll be awake to know.

Darkness surrounds the train. Now and then a road is illuminated by flashing red lights as we speed through railroad crossings, train horn howling. At night, far from home, the howl sounds sadder than usual.

The town of Tunnel City just flashed past. We are near the Wisconsin-Minnesota border.

"Driving Miss Daisy," is playing in the lounge car. I can always watch a movie. I'd rather sit here in the dark car looking out.

I just saw a man, wearing an undershirt, sitting in his living room with the lights out. He was illuminated by television glow. That's a common sight at night from a train.

Communities are whizzing by. I don't have enough interest to get out the map to check their names.

These are the one-horse, middle-of-nowhere, jerkwater, don't-blink-or-you'll-miss-them towns everybody jokes about.

More television glows. Soon it will be time for the late night TV news programs, something not available on trains. Long-distance passengers are cut off from much of what's going on in the outside world.

Telephones will come to trains such as the Empire Builder before long, maybe even TV. I'm not sure that's so good.

There's something to be said for being out of touch, cutting ties, breaking the routine -- at least for short periods of time.

For now, though, the only outside contact for people on this train is the radio.

My Walkman is on. Dialed-in voices drift in and out, like people you meet on trains.

"When you need answers," says a male voice from some station, "come to your credit union."

Thanks, buddy, but the answers most of us need aren't found in credit unions.

A slight move of the dial. "This is K106-FM. My name is Mary Price and this is Hank Williams Junior with 'Ain't Misbehavin'."

I ain't misbehavin' either. There ain't nobody here to misbehave with.

Down the radio dial a preacher is trying to save souls. "A whole new world will open for you when you accept the Lord Jesus as your personal savior."

I don't know if the woman in the compartment across the hall needs saving, but she might need help.

She was crying when she boarded in Chicago and is still crying. She takes meals in her room, which is the only time she opens the compartment's curtains.

There are other troubles on this train. A woman lost a purse containing $1,700 in cash and a lot of jewelry at the station in

Chicago. She was talking about it earlier tonight in the lounge car. She said what most of us have said at one time or another.

"It isn't so much the money. It's all the things that can't be replaced."

Somebody else in the lounge car has problems of another sort. His lady friend left him and moved to Seattle. He is going there, even though he doesn't know her address.

"I'll find her, and I'm gonna do my best to get her back."

Seattle is a big place. What if she can't be found. What if he does find her and she won't have him back? I didn't ask either question.

Out in the corridor, a tour group guide is chewing out the sleeping car attendant. She says his service hasn't been good, but gives him a tip anyway.

I tune in "River City's KG-95, the station for yesterday's favorites," according to the female disc jockey.

She puts on an old Bee Gees song. The words remind me of the fellow in the lounge car, the one going to Seattle in search of his lady friend.

"Here we are in a room full of strangers...Well, I had to follow you, though you did not want me to...I can't stay away..."

The Empire Builder's horn howls again as we pass another nothing-more-than-a-wide-spot-in-the-road town. Most buildings are dark now, except for the ones with neon Pabst and Bud signs in the window and a few cars out front.

We will make North Dakota by morning.

The woman across the hall is still crying.

Wisconsin Man Finds Safe Haven in Rockies

East Glacier Park, MT -- Richard Clauson, age 61, was using the telephone inside the Beaded Spear Gift Shop, one of 12 businesses lining U.S. 2, which goes through the middle of town. That's where I saw him for the first time.

When he hung up the phone, Pat Lee, who owns the store with her husband, said, "Richard, would you watch things for a few minutes?"

Richard said he would and she left to run errands.

I was surprised to hear Richard still talking because I was the store's only customer. For several minutes he carried on quite a conversation with himself, stopping only when he saw me looking.

"Don't mind me," he said. "I've had a brain injury."

Never at a loss for words, I said, "Oh."

"I'm OK, though," he quickly added in a high-pitched, sing-song voice.

I said that was good.

"Are you enjoying your vacation?" Richard asked.

Pretending that I was on vacation seemed easier than explaining I was riding trains around the country to gather information to write stories. Besides, most people think that's a vacation, and they might have a point.

"I'm glad you are having a good time," Richard said. "I'm glad you are here."

His was my first welcome to Montana.

"I'm glad you didn't come last month," Richard said. "We had two weeks of rain. Cold rain. I'm glad you weren't here then. I'm glad you are here now, though. This is the most beautiful place in the world."

Brain injury or not, Richard would make the Chamber of Commerce proud.

"I live right up there," Richard said. He was pointing to woods at the foot of the Rocky Mountains, which begin here. Richard's house is just west of Glacier Park Lodge, which closed a few days ago on Labor Day, and won't reopen until June 1.

The tourist season here is short. Winter comes early and stays late. Snowbanks are still here in May, I've been told.

Pat Lee and her husband, Al, returned.

"They are my guardian angels," Richard said.

He then headed to Lowry's Diner. He said he wanted a cup of coffee.

I watched him walk right past the coffee shop. He forgot to stop.

Seconds later he did stop. He slapped his forehead with the palm of his hand, turned and walked back to the diner. He was smiling and talking to himself.

I could almost hear him say, "I have a brain injury, but I'm OK."

Richard lives in beauty. The town of East Glacier is at an entrance to the 1.5-million acre Glacier National Park.

The permanent population is about 200. It swells to nobody-knows-what in summer.

East Glacier, elevation about 4,500 feet, has long and hard winters. They say the winds are brutal.

Al Lee recalls the time railroad freight cars were parked on the tracks near the Amtrak station.

"Wind blew the cars right over," Al said.

There isn't much to town. You can jog from end to end in two or three minutes. There are a couple places to eat, drink, sleep and buy supplies.

I had lunch, walked around town and went back to the Beaded Spear. Al was giving directions to a tourist.

When he finished, I said, "Tell me about Richard Clauson."

"Well, he has had a brain injury. There was an auto wreck," Al said and continued.

"He was here many years ago and liked it and came back to live six years ago. He pulled everything he owned in a wagon all the way from Green Bay, Wisconsin."

I said, "He managed to fit everything he owned in a station wagon?"

Al shook his head "no" and smiled.

"A child's wagon. He walked here all the way from Green Bay pulling a wagon. He's a remarkable man."

Al led me out the store's back door.

"When he comes to town for supplies, he brings his wagon. He leaves it in the back here. He's quite proud of that wagon."

The wagon was gone. Al said it was just like a regular kid's wagon except it had bigger wheels.

I asked Al why Richard called him and Pat his guardian angels.

Al said they helped Richard build his one-room house in the woods.

"For the first two years he lived in a tent."

I thought of mountain winds blowing over railroad cars, temperatures of 40 below and a man in a tent.

When Richard, who lives on a small disability pension, wanted to build his house, he came to Al. He needed money for materials and Al co-signed a loan.

"I didn't worry," Al said. "We trust him. His handshake is good."

Al said Richard's house was built on Indian land. The Blackfeet have leased an acre to Richard for 25 years at no charge.

I've just returned from Richard's house in the woods. There is no running water, furnace or electricity and only one room, but it's big enough for someone living alone.

Richard built it on a hill near a clear stream. He showed me the road he cut, the berries he picks, the beaver dams in his front yard and the Rocky Mountains out back.

And he showed me his seven dogs, which came to him from several sources and in various conditions.

"The Lord sent them to me," Richard said. "He wants me to take care of them. Isn't this a beautiful place?"

Yes, I thought, East Glacier Park is a beautiful place and I am talking to one of the reasons why that is true.

Derailed Train Slows the Trip, But Doesn't Stop It

Aboard the Empire Builder -- The children's story about the "little engine that could" comes to mind as two engines, each with 1,300 horsepower, pulls us higher into Washington's Cascade Mountains.

The track curves back and forth along the side of the mountain as we continue the crawling climb.

The moment we enter the 7.8-mile Cascade Tunnel, the longest railroad tunnel in the Western Hemisphere, I will push the button on my stopwatch.

I just did.

The sun, blue sky, pine trees, mountains and an occasional glimpse of highway have been replaced with total blackness. I won't bother turning on lights. The tunnel's blackness is good for thinking back to things I've done and people I've met during the past few days, which is what I will do.

The Empire Builder, train number 7, had been scheduled to arrive at 7:42 last night in East Glacier Park, Montana. The stop lasts less than a minute.

Five of us were waiting in East Glacier's rustic train station, built of brown painted logs. Three of us were passengers. The other two, a man and woman, were Amtrak employees who work there.

"The train will be late," said the male employee. "There has been a derailment east of here."

He explained that a freight was blocking all train traffic and that the Empire Builder would arrive about two hours late.

Joe and Doris, the other two passengers, shifted positions and tried to get comfortable on the waiting room bench.

They live in Los Angeles, paid $30,000 for a home now worth $200,000, have a business that involves coin operated washing machines, own a second home in Palm Springs, were once in Glens Falls, NY, the nearest they ever got to Utica, and were now heading home after a long vacation.

They told me those things after knowing me for less than five minutes.

I left my bag in the waiting room with Joe and Doris and crossed the street to the Park Bar. Two hours late would probably mean three hours.

The Park serves Rainier Beer, sells Tombstone Pizza, has an electronic card game and a pool table. Taped on the wall behind the bar is a list of five people no longer welcome in the bar. There had been six names but one was crossed out.

Getting barred from this bar is something to worry about. There aren't any other bars here.

Two construction workers at the bar's far end were arguing with their boss about pay.

"One punch and I'm out of here," said a guy two stools from me.

I just stared at myself in the back bar mirror. Sometimes you are better off that way.

Two Indian women, probably Blackfeet, were discussing personal matters, but in voices that made it impossible not to overhear.

"I heard about your, uh, incident," said the thin one. "What really happened?"

"He punched me out," said the heavier one, who had symbols of some sort tattooed on her hand, "knocked me clear across the room."

Both of them laughed. I wondered why.

I left an empty bottle of Rainier and a tip and went up the street to the Villager Restaurant. I had to wait for a table. The food is good, and it's the only eating place in East Glacier open after 8 p.m.

Any thought of the train arriving within two hours disappeared. Both Amtrak agents were having dinner and taking their time.

"Looks like it will be closer to three hours late," said the female agent.

I asked where letters could be mailed.

"Right here," she said. Her dinner companion was the postmaster.

The restaurant was all couples, except for me and a woman eating alone across the room. Both of us were writing in notebooks with one hand and eating with the other.

I wondered what she was writing and I wondered if she wondered the same about me.

I ordered a big meal. The Empire Builder's dining car wouldn't be open until tomorrow for breakfast.

It was in the dining car, two days ago, that I met a couple from Elgin, Illinois, Mr. and Mrs. Ballew.

"Just remember a ball," he said, "and add an e-w."

I had the feeling that Mr. Ball e-w had spoken those exact words to thousands of people over the years.

Mr. Ballew prayed before starting in on his eggs. Mr. Ballew got through heart surgery not long ago and credits the Lord.

Mr. Ballew, a retired machinist, 32 years with International Harvester, is praying harder than usual these days. His daughter, who lives in Seattle, will soon undergo brain surgery.

"It is being written up in a medical journal," Mr. Ballew said.

Sun just filled my sleeping compartment. We are out of the Cascade Tunnel.

According to my watch, we were in there for 16 minutes, 22 seconds. It seemed longer.

Train Stories Come to Life While Riding The Rails

Aboard the California Zephyr -- We've left Chicago far behind. The 14-car train is quiet, except for soothing clicking sounds from metal wheels on metal rails.

The land is flat and without trees, making it easy to see zigzags of electricity touch ground. In a few minutes it will be dark. The lightning will be all the more spectacular.

Just now, the flat land was interrupted by a farmhouse, around which are barns, sheds and trees.

From my compartment, which is No. 5 in sleeping car 32048, I can hear people gasp at particularly brilliant bolts. I wonder what would happen if the Zephyr is struck.

I can also hear the fellow in compartment No. 8. His curtain is closed, but the sliding door is not. The man has a wealth of information about trains and is sharing some with his kids. Lucky kids.

Now, just before their bedtime, he is reading the kids a Carl Sandburg story about a hobo riding the rails. As I said, lucky kids.

It's a good story. I put down my book, get comfortable and listen. The man in compartment No. 8 has a good voice for reading out loud.

I'm hoping the kids don't fall asleep. I'd like their father to continue. I'm enjoying this.

They stayed awake for a long time.

The next afternoon is when we started the long climb up from Denver through the Rocky Mountains. There are 42 tunnels, including the six-mile long Moffat Tunnel.

We crossed the Continental Divide at 9,239 feet and went through Rollins Pass. There are deep patches of snow. In four days it will be May.

The observation car is packed with people taking pictures. They might as well save their energy. No picture can capture this beauty.

I wait until later in the day, when the views aren't quite so exciting, before striking up a conversation with the man in compartment No. 8.

His name is Terry Pindell, 41, of Keene, NH.

I ask, "How is it that you know so much about trains?"

He answers, "I've ridden every Amtrak train in America at least once, some several times."

Pindell says that a year ago, between January and June, he rode 35,000 rail miles gathering material for a soon-to-be published book called "Making Tracks."

"There are 17 chapters in the book," Pindell says. "There are 17 long distance Amtrak trains. One chapter for every train."

The bearded, pipe-smoking, former English professor at Middlebury College in Vermont said he quit teaching to write articles and books.

This, however, is a pleasure trip. He and his wife, Nancy, a librarian, and their two kids are going to San Francisco.

I ask about his book.

"It's not strictly a railroad book. It's Americana. It's travel. It is not a book just for railroad buffs."

The book will contain several stories about people Pindell met during his six months on trains.

There was, for example, a mysterious lady who handed out $20 bills to strangers, a drug courier who was arrested when he left the train, a woman with two husbands, and an Irish couple in this country illegally.

"You never know what interesting people you're liable to meet on a train," Pindell said.

I'm looking at him and thinking the same thing.

Pindell has even seen a suicide. A 33-year-old man waited until the Sunset Limited, a train which runs through the southwest, was close and then laid down on the tracks.

Pindell interviewed the engineer.

"There was no way he could have stopped in time," Pindell said as he shook his head. "These suicides are more common than people think."

Ruby Canyon and the Colorado-Utah border are just ahead. Pindell goes back to his room to share the view with his family.

Tonight, as the Zephyr rushes through the darkness of Utah, Pindell will read his kids to sleep again. On tap is a Mark Twain story about riding the train to San Francisco.

I can't wait.

It's 'Westward, ho' After a Close Encounter

Aboard the Southwest Chief -- We are in Colorado, somewhere in the Sangre de Cristo Mountains.

The Chief's speed has dropped to a crawl as she pulls hard up the 7,588 feet to Raton Pass, the highest point on the route west. We are following the old Santa Fe Trail, parts of which are still visible.

Ahead, according to the Amtrak route guide, are the ruins of Clifton House, once a layover point on the Santa Fe Trail, and Fort Union, built in 1851 to guard the trail.

I'm sitting in an observation car. We just passed a ghost town, and what's left of a Spanish mission, cross still intact.

"Beautiful country," I remark to the guy across the aisle.

"Sure is," he says without looking up from the video game he has played for the past hundred miles.

Early this morning, just after leaving Dodge City, the land was flat. The tallest things were grain elevators like the one we passed in Garden City, Kansas. I'm told it's the largest in the world.

Garden City also claims the largest free public swimming pool and the largest buffalo herd in the country. Neither can be seen from the train, though.

The train just went dark as we entered the half-mile tunnel at Raton Pass on the Colorado border. The darkness reminds me of this morning and how I nearly missed catching the train at Dodge City.

It wasn't my fault, though. I'll tell you what happened.

There are several places to spend the night in Dodge, modern motels with familiar names.

But Dodge has a special old hotel with charm and character, The Lora-Locke. The hotel is in the center of town at the corner of Central and Gunsmoke and looks like something out of the 1920's, which is when it was built.

"I think you'll enjoy it," said the Amtrak man at the train station, responding to my lodging inquiries.

"They just put in new bedding. There's a good bar and restaurant. The place is clean and cheap. Errol Flynn once stayed there."

The Lora-Locke was just as described. And I discovered that Errol Flynn wasn't the only big name to stay there. The Lora-Locke has provided rooms for Ann Sheridan, Joel McCrea, Olivia DeHaviland and Gunsmoke's Amanda Blake.

My stay at The Lora-Locke was uneventful until before dawn this morning, which is when I was supposed to leave my fourth floor room and head for the train station.

The electricity went out at the same time the telephone went dead. I waited as long as I dared, but the lights didn't come back on. More by touch than sight, I packed my suitcase and headed into the corridor. I had a train to catch.

The emergency lights in the hall were also out. By touching the wall, I made it to the elevator, which wasn't working. It was too dark to find the stairs.

Thank goodness for the lady I met quite by chance. She was standing at the other end of the hall holding a lighted match at arm's length in front of her face.

The match went out. She struck another.

She looked to be in her early 20s, and wore a white cowboy hat, a white western style shirt with sequins and a red scarf, knotted at the side of her neck.

She was probably wearing tight jeans and pointy-toe, high-heeled cowboy boots, too. I couldn't tell. The match went out before I could look. We were standing next to each other in the dark.

Since she had matches, I told her I wouldn't mind staying with her and trying to find the stairs to the lobby.

No problem, she said, adding that she was quite familiar with the hotel.

I explained that time was of the essence, though, since I was supposed to have left for the station 10 minutes earlier and if I missed the train I was in trouble.

"Darlin', I'm the one in trouble," she said. "I was supposed to have been home last night."

"Oh," I said.

I got to the station just as the Chief was ready to pull out. How the cowgirl made out when she got home, I have no idea.

The Chief just came out of the tunnel at the western end of Raton Pass and the sun is pouring through the windows again. We are in New Mexico, westerly bound.

Winnemucca: More Than Spot on Map

Winnemucca, NV -- The train arrived near dawn, and stopped here for less than one minute. Nobody got off except me.

Snow was coming down hard, but it melted on contact. I walked down Melarkey Street toward distant neon lights, the only sign of life.

I stopped in Winnemucca because I wanted to see a town different than the one people usually stop at when visiting Nevada. Besides, the town's name caught my fancy.

I walked through the front door of Winners Hotel and Casino, whose neon had guided me here.

There is life in Winnemucca even at this early hour. It is in the casino.

Standing around the room pumping nickels, dimes, quarters and dollars into machines with unending appetites is a cross section of America.

There are six casinos, including Winners, which is where I met Charlie Hastings.

He was there when I arrived at dawn. He was there when I returned after dark. He hadn't moved from his spot overlooking the dice table.

We talked for a few minutes. I asked about his luck. He laughed the way people do when it's either laugh or cry.

"The gambling bug eats you up," he said. "It lets you win enough to keep you alive. You'd be better off if it didn't."

If Charlie Hastings is to be believed, he has lost his wife, children, house and several jobs because of his gambling.

Out the casino's front door and to the left is a place for people such as Charlie Hastings. It's a place to sell your watch, jewelry, wedding band, and anything else worth cash.

Credit is something you don't get much of in gambling towns. The stuffed bear in the Sundance Casino on Winnemucca Boulevard makes that point.

"If you want credit," says the sign, "ask the bear. If he winks, you get the credit."

I asked the woman behind the bar if the bear ever winked.

"Hardly ever," she said, "hardly ever."

Her name is Joni Marrelli. She says Winnemucca is a boom town. I've heard the same thing from several people.

"It's the gold mines," she said. "So many people are coming in here it's hard to find a place to live."

Houses are in short supply, but jobs aren't.

"If you can't find a job in a day or two here," she said, "something is wrong with you."

I thought of Charlie Hastings. He told me he tried but couldn't find a job.

Near the Sundance is the Humboldt County Library, where I learned that the town is named after Winnemucca, a Paiute chief.

Although a small town, Winnemucca has a museum, art gallery, golf course, bowling alley, theater and five houses of prostitution, which is legal in this county.

Those houses, I'm told, are one reason Winnemucca attracts conventions. The houses are grouped together in the Baud Street area of town, out of sight, but less than five minutes from the casinos, the other convention attraction.

"There is more to Winnemucca than meets the eye," said Hughie Schoff.

I wasn't sure if he was referring to the out of sight houses on Baud Street. Before I could ask, he was talking about food.

Schoff sat at the bar in the Martin Hotel, which features an excellent restaurant. There is a large Basque settlement in Winnemucca and the Martin is famous for Basque food.

Basque festivals, western celebrations, hunting and fishing are the things that Schoff likes to talk about, which stands to reason considering he is director of Winnemucca's Convention and Visitors Bureau.

He said the town was perfect for conventions of up to 500 people. A convention of that size is in town right now, lady bowlers.

"In Las Vegas they'd get lost in the crowd," Schoff said. "Here they own the town."

Schoff answered numerous questions and asked just one. He wanted to know if I'd gone to any of the casinos and how I'd done.

I told him I'd lost $30.

"Son," he said, "if you just lost $30, you won."

Items Of Interest

I've just returned from a train trip. I noted these items:

ITEM -- The most common name for a business in San Antonio is Alamo. Look in the telephone book and you'll see Alamo Plumbing, Alamo Taxi, Alamo Cleaners, Alamo Apartments, Alamo Liquors, Alamo Heating, Alamo Printing, Alamo Plumbing...You probably get the point. By the way, they are building a domed stadium in San Antonio. I'll let you guess its name.

ITEM -- According to my unscientific survey, Washington, D.C. has more uniformed guards, more U.S. flags, more statues, more metal detectors, more joggers and more memorials than any city in the country. One of the newest memorials is the Vietnam Veterans Memorial. Near it is a tent occupied by veterans. They call it the "POW-MIA Vigil at the Wall". Veterans have been there 24 hours a day since Nov. 11, 1982, and will stay "until they all come home".

ITEM -- One of the most popular displays at Washington's Smithsonian Museum of American History is the one containing the red shoes worn by Judy Garland in "The Wizard of Oz."

ITEM -- Specialty drinks can be found in every city. Included in the ones offered in Santa Barbara are the Santa Barbara Sunset (tequila, Grand Marnier, orange juice, grenadine), Screaming Banshee (creme de banana, cacao, vodka, banana, ice cream), Santa Barbara Iced Tea (vodka, rum, gin, Triple Sec, cranberry juice, 7-Up).

ITEM -- A New York City man, who said he hadn't eaten since the day before, offered to carry my bag from one side of Penn Station to the other for the "price of a cup of coffee and a donut." When we got there he said, "That will be $4.95." We negotiated it down to $1.50. I told him he'd have to start frequenting cheaper coffee shops.

ITEM -- The Lake Shore Limited passes through Ossining, NY, home to Sing Sing Correctional Facility. A reason for building a prison at Ossining was so prisoners from New York City could easily be transported up the Hudson River, which originated a famous saying. To be sent "up the river" meant getting sent to Sing Sing.

ITEM -- The Lake Shore Limited also passes through Beacon, NY, which got its name because of the signal fires that once burned on nearby mountains to warn Colonial forces of British advances up the Hudson River.

ITEM -- Despite its comparatively small population, Utica, NY has one of the best looking train stations in the United States.

Nothing Beats Southern Hospitality

Charlottesville, VA -- It's nice to be greeted when you get off a train after a long ride.

I got off Amtrak's Crescent, which brought me here from New Orleans. A dozen or so of us got off. Everybody had somebody waiting for them at the depot.

This was my first time in Charlottesville. I didn't know anyone.

But Tom Cosner was there to greet me.

"Welcome, sir," he said, "I would be happy to drive you wherever you'd like to go. Please call me Tom."

He said this as he held open the door to a 1976 Chevrolet, which is the entire Terminal Cab Company fleet.

"I have a couple hundred thousand miles on it," he said. "She still runs pretty good. I put 175,000 miles on the first engine and I have 40,000 on this motor."

Tom is the owner and only employee of the Terminal Cab Co. Tom was once one of 15 employees, but cabs aren't needed in Charlottesville as much as they once were.

"Most of the old boys I used to drive with are dead and gone."

Years ago, when the owner of the Terminal Cab Co. wanted to get out of the business, he sold the name and two cabs to Tom.

Tom said he started providing rides to people here in 1941.

"The kids at the college (University of Virginia) don't hardly believe me when I tell them I used to haul students from the train depot up to the college for 25 cents."

The price hasn't increased all that much. Tom now charges $3.50.

I told Tom to pick out the place he would choose if he was spending the night in Charlottesville and to take me there.

On the way, Tom, age 70, who will be married 50 years come November, was saying he had planned on retiring a few years back, but the money he set aside wasn't enough anymore.

"My plans done backfired, so I come out here to make a few bucks to keep my head above water. I'm not complaining, understand. I've made a decent living and sleep well and eat well. You can't take even a dime with you when you go, anyway."

I suspect, however, that Tom would be out here driving his cab even if he didn't need the money.

"Well, sir, you meet some wonderful people and interesting people, too. I stay away from mean looking people and I don't fiddle around nights anymore."

A telephone number is painted on the side of Tom's cab. I told Tom I'd give him a call if I needed a cab during my stay.

"Calling that number won't help much," Tom said. "That's my house. Nobody's there during the day."

I asked how he got customers if there was no way to reach him.

"My regular customers call me at night and let me know if they want to go somewhere the next day, and I meet the train every morning and go to the bus depot. That's good enough."

Tom dropped me at a clean, moderately priced motel near the university and handed me the end flap from a cigarette carton, on which he had written Terminal Taxi, the date, the amount of the fare and his signature.

I noticed that he had a stack of end flaps in the front seat.

Later in the day, the telephone in my motel room rang.

"Just wanted to see if you needed to get anywhere," Tom said.

I said I'd like to get out to Thomas Jefferson's Monticello. Tom drove me out and waited while I took the tour.

"I'll just sit here and wait for you," Tom said. "No extra charge."

How many cab drivers do you know who will do that?

"Take your time inside," Tom said. "Be sure to see everything," which I did.

Tom took the long way back to the motel to show me downtown Charlottesville and some of its historic buildings.

"If you need anything tonight, call me at home," Tom said. "I'll be glad to help you anyway I can."

I said I would.

"I hope you enjoy our town. Most people do. I don't know what we've got here, but people just seem to fall in love with our little town."

Maybe it's something called Southern hospitality.

Cemeteries

Charlottesville, VA -- Monticello, the beautiful hilltop home of Thomas Jefferson, is owned and operated by a private, non-profit organization that provides tours. Monticello is pronounced Mont-ti-chello. I'm told that means "little mountain" in Italian.

Admission to Monticello is $7. I gave them a $10 bill and got a $1 and $2 bill in change. They go through stacks of brand new crisp $2 bills at Monticello.

"We're probably the only place in the country using them," the ticket taker said.

Which is quite appropriate considering whose picture appears on $2 bills.

Jefferson is buried down the road from his house. The graveyard is still being used for his descendants, which number about 1,200.

Jefferson left special instructions on what was to be inscribed on his tombstone. These are the words he wanted:

"Here was buried Thomas Jefferson
Author of the Declaration of American Independence
Of the Statute of Virginia for Religious Freedom
And Father of the University of Virginia."

I thought it odd that Jefferson didn't put anything on his tombstone about being president of the United States.

Speaking of tombstones and epitaphs, someone I know swears he saw this one chiseled into a tombstone out west:

Here lies Pecos Bill
He always lied
And he always will;
He once lied loud
He now lies still.

There are other epitaphs I haven't seen in my travels. I don't expect I ever will.

On a hotel clerk's tombstone:	"Checked Out."
On a postal worker's:	"Canceled."
On a prizefighter's:	"KO'ed."
On a hypochondriac's:	"I Told You I Was Sick."
On a carpenter's:	"Dead As A Doornail."
On a baseball player's:	"Strike Three."
On a movie director's:	"The End."
On a magician's:	"Vanished Into Thin Air."
On a basketball player's:	"Fouled Out."
On a gambler's:	"Out Of Luck."
On a pilot's:	"Final Approach."
On a chess player's:	"Good Knight."
On a mechanic's:	"Out Of Gas."
On a radio operator's:	"Over And Out."
On a drummer's:	"Deadbeat."
On a good elevator operator's:	"Going Up."
On a good-for-nothing elevator operator's:	"Going Down."
On a hiker's:	"End of the Trail."

On a gardener's:	"Transplanted."
On an astronaut's:	"Lost In Space."
On a New Yorker's:	"Taxed To Death."
On a funeral director's:	"My Turn."
On a blackjack player's:	"Busted."

On the Rails With Dreams of Past, Future

Aboard the Sunset Limited -- We pulled out of Union Station in Los Angeles last night at 11 and stopped for a minute this morning in Phoenix, then Tucson.

San Antonio is a day and night up the line.

We are somewhere between Lordsburg and Deming, NM. The terrain is flat and uninteresting.

According to the announcement just made, we have crossed the Continental Divide. Waters east of the Divide flow into the Atlantic. Waters to its west go to the Pacific.

The lounge car is filled with couples and groups. One man is sitting alone. I saw him get on in Los Angeles.

His name is Marvin Buckert. He is 62, lives in San Antonio, and recently retired. He used to drive the train we are now riding.

"Some of the guys I worked with said I'd be dead a week after I retired, " Buckert said, "but I'm enjoying myself."

Buckert was returning from a visit to California.

"I get to ride the train for free."

But he can't do that too often because his wife has medical problems and can't travel. Besides, his parents are quite elderly.

He has a daughter, who is a nurse, and a son.

"He's an engineer for Southern Pacific. He's damned good, too. The guys told me, 'Hell, he handles a train as good as you ever did.'"

Marvin Buckert started on the railroad at age 17 as a laborer and dreamed of becoming an engineer. He worked his way up and hauled freight for Southern Pacific and then passengers for Amtrak.

For a year or two before his retirement, Buckert was senior engineer in his division. He could pick his routes and the pay was more than he thought he'd ever earn.

"I felt like a millionaire. I felt better than a millionaire. I was in heaven."

But it wasn't all good. Buckert's train killed a man once. The man's legs were spread across the tracks west of San Antonio.

"I couldn't stop in time. It was on a curve. I didn't see him until it was too late."

Buckert continued, "I never did find out what he was doing there. I don't know whether he was drunk or drugged or if somebody hit him on the head."

Then there was the time a woman and her son were in a stalled car on the tracks. Buckert managed to stop in time, but it was close.

"She had a bottle in the car. She was drunk."

While Buckert was relaxing in the lounge car, waitress Amy King was working in the dining car.

Between meals, when the dining car is empty, I've seen King sitting alone in a booth with a sketch book and pens.

An artist?

She hesitated before answering.

"I'm never sure whether to say 'yes' or 'no' when somebody asks me that question. I hate to say 'yes' because I'm struggling, but that's my dream."

She is 23, has two years of a Los Angeles art school under her belt and one of these days is going back to take more classes.

"It isn't easy for me. I want something to come out one way, but it comes out looking like something else."

She took eating utensils, which would be used for dinner, and rolled them in napkins while we talked.

"I have a great boyfriend, though. He works for an art supply company. He has been real supportive."

King said she was doing an apprenticeship with a Los Angeles artist.

"He has been making a living at it for ten years. I've been meeting a lot of other artists who are making a living. That's all I'd like to do is be able to make a living."

At dinner, Marvin Buckert was assigned to one of Amy King's tables. I saw them smile at each other, but they didn't talk.

He didn't know she had a dream. She didn't know he had achieved his.

Musings From the Road

Pearl Scarbough of Nashville, a retired school teacher, and her husband, Fred, have traveled throughout the United States and to many countries around the world.

I met them on the California Zephyr. They were on their way to Reno.

When she said they had never once had a bad trip, I asked for their secret.

"It's all in your attitude," Pearl said. "Some people start off a trip looking for things to complain about. They might as well stay at home because they will find them. We don't complain about every little thing that goes wrong. We don't let things bother us. We try to be positive."

Apparently they use that philosophy in other parts of their life. They have been married 50 years and have no intention of changing that arrangement in the foreseeable future.

I observed the Scarboughs for many miles on the Zephyr. Too bad everybody isn't so happy.

I've observed several other things while traveling around the United States on one train or another. These are a few of those observations:

- Some people take pride in their communities. A popular bumper sticker in Utica, Michigan: "I Love Utica."

- I wouldn't have believed it if I hadn't been there, but going through Utah it was raining on one side of the train and dry on the other.

- Winnemucca, Nevada, with a population of less than 10,000, is uncrowded and that's the way they like it, which might explain a bumper sticker I saw there: "One Traffic Jam Every Decade in Winnemucca."

- At the Utica Packing Company in Utica, Michigan, they slaughter 8,000 pigs a day. Most of the meat goes to New York.

- If ever in Winnemucca, Nevada stop at the Martin Hotel for a wonderful drink called Picon Punch, which the Basques there make and enjoy. They caution, however, that drinking too many will cause you to forget where you are. Continuing to drink them will cause you to forget who you are. I guess that's right. I can't remember.

- People of all ages wave at trains. People on trains wave back. They always have. They always will. It's one of the rules of the universe.

- In Glenwood Springs, Colorado, a hermit lives in a cave on the side of a mountain. Train passengers can see the man standing outside his cave. He doesn't wave. There are exceptions to every rule of the universe.

- A cowboy by the name of Phil Tobin once represented the northern part of Nevada in the state assembly. A great many people owe a debt of gratitude to that cowboy. He was the one who decades ago introduced the legislation to legalize gambling in Nevada.

- There is a great looking train station, complete with clock tower, in Niles, Michigan. The station was built in 1891. Having a nice looking railroad station says something good about a community.

Difference Between Day, Night at Alamo

San Antonio, TX -- As soon as I checked into a hotel here, I got a street map and headed to the Alamo.

I can't remember when I wasn't interested in the Alamo. When I was a boy, I read every Alamo book in the library.

And with millions of other children who grew up in the 1950s, my hero was Davy Crockett, the one portrayed by Fess Parker and promoted by Walt Disney.

I grew up, but didn't lose my interest in the Alamo and the people who fought there. The facts, I discovered, were better than Hollywood fiction.

There's no way to improve on the actions of Col. William Travis, who drew a line in the Texas dirt with his sword. Those willing to die for freedom should cross the line, Travis said.

The men at the Alamo crossed over, knowing what was going to happen. There were 189 of them. The Mexican general, Santa Anna, had an army of 4,000.

Only one man in the Alamo decided against crossing the line. From him, we know the others did. Even Jim Bowie, sick with pneumonia, asked that his cot be carried over the line.

For years I've looked forward to seeing the Alamo. And now, according to the street map, I was close.

Two couples stopped me on the way and asked directions to the Alamo. I showed them my map, which we really didn't need. Get within a couple blocks of the Alamo and follow the crowd.

I walked up Villita Street, went left on Navarro, cut through a park and there was the Alamo.

It comes on you without warning. You don't expect to find the Alamo in the heart of downtown San Antonio surrounded by F.W. Woolworth, Wendy's, Burger King, Alamo Shirts, Time Out Amusement Center, Ripley's Believe It Or Not, Alamo Optical, The Theater of Wax, Pizza Hut and the Crockett Hotel.

The Alamo is much smaller than I had imagined, and looks even smaller than it is because of the surrounding tall buildings.

"I was expecting more," a man in the crowd said.

I couldn't see his face. I was blocked by a camera. The street was filled with picture takers.

In the small park fronting the Alamo, Brother Charlie, a street preacher, was shouting to a crowd that wasn't listening. He shared the park with people selling craft items and cold drinks.

I walked to the Alamo's front door. A sign asked visitors to be quiet inside, to refrain from taking pictures and to remove hats.

Many visitors must not have seen the sign.

No admission is charged, although there are containers for people wanting to make donations. Some do.

Inside are relics such as Davy Crockett's fork, beaded buckskin vest, razor and a lock of his hair.

Davy is clearly the star of the Alamo. His portrait, painted while he was still living, according to the sign, hangs in a place of prominence.

Davy doesn't look anything like Fess Parker or John Wayne. Davy doesn't even look formidable.

I asked an Alamo guide how many people tour the building.

"Three and a half million a year," the guide said.

There's a souvenir shop connected to the Alamo by a walk. They don't, I am happy to report, allow souvenir selling in the Alamo itself.

I spent an hour in the Alamo. When I came out into the bright sun, Brother Charlie was gone, replaced by another street preacher, not nearly as good. Nobody was paying attention to him, either.

I went to dinner. It was dark when I started back to the hotel. If I took the long way, I would pass the Alamo. I took the long way. I had no place else to go.

The Alamo was different now. The shops were closed. The street preachers were gone. The vendors had left the park. There wasn't a person or camera in sight.

The Alamo was softly illuminated. It stood out in the dark and was the first thing to catch your eye, the way it should be, the way I had hoped it would be.

"Looks better this way, doesn't it?" a man's voice said.

A man and woman were sitting in the park. I hadn't seen them when I arrived.

I agreed that it was better now.

Cab Lingo to be Wary of: 'Don't Worry'

San Antonio, TX -- There are three signs to indicate a less than reliable cab driver.

Be wary when:

1. The driver drives with one hand and has a street map in the other.

2. The driver gets to an intersection, looks both ways and says, "H'mmm."

3. The driver looks worried but tells you not to worry.

Juan, a happy looking man in his early 20s, arrived at the hotel, loaded my bag in the trunk and said, "Where to, mister?"

"Train station," I said. "I've got 20 minutes to catch my train."

At this point I should tell you that the cab driver who picked me up on my arrival in San Antonio took less than 10 minutes to drive to the very same hotel I was now leaving.

Juan pulled out a street map, took a long look and pulled away from the curb.

"Don't worry," Juan said, "I'll get you there in plenty of time."

Juan drove four blocks, stopped at a red light, looked both ways, and said, "H'mmm."

He then held a microphone close to his mouth and said, "Nineteen to base. Could you tell me what street the railroad station is on?"

The dispatcher laughed and said, "Juan, are you lost again?"

Right then I should have known I had a less than reliable cab driver.

Juan denied being lost.

"I just wanted to make sure," the dispatcher said.

Juan took another look at his map. I pulled out my map.

I was fairly sure Juan was headed in the wrong direction. I told him so.

"No, mister," he said, "this is the way. I am pretty sure."

His "pretty" sure was stronger than my "fairly" sure, but I was worried. Nothing looked familiar.

The train was scheduled to leave in 16 minutes. I finally told Juan I was sure he was going the wrong way and to turn around.

"Mister, please be patient. I was there once."

"That makes us even, Juan. I was there once, too. And I was there more recently than you. Turn around. The train leaves in 14 minutes."

"I'll get you there," said Juan, who hadn't been smiling for the past few blocks. "Don't worry."

I swore at Juan and demanded that he radio his dispatcher, admit to being lost and ask for directions.

Juan could no longer speak English.

I used what I could remember of my high school Spanish.

"El Amtrako stationo in 12 minutoes or you one dead hombre."

Juan refused to respond. I took matters into my own hands and reached across the front seat for the microphone. I would have gotten it, too, if Juan hadn't hung a hard right, causing me to lose my balance.

"Look, mister," said Juan, who suddenly remembered English, "there it is. I told you not to worry."

It was still dark, but I could see an engine, tracks and railroad cars a few blocks ahead.

Good old Juan came through after all. He got me here with four or five minutes to spare. I apologized for swearing at him and said I would make it up to him with good tip.

I was especially grateful since Juan was going the wrong way on a one way street, explaining as he went that it would take too long to go around. It was good of Juan to risk his life, my life and his company's car to get me there on time.

It took another block to see that Juan's heroics were in vain. He had taken me to Southern Pacific's freight terminal.

I swore at Juan again, pounded the seat and told him to radio for help.

Juan admitted defeat and called his dispatcher.

"I knew you were lost again, Juan," the laughing dispatcher said.

At least one person in the group was having fun.

The dispatcher stayed on the radio and talked Juan into the Amtrak station. We arrived four minutes late.

"What about my tip, mister Joe?" Juan asked as he handed over my bag.

Juan learned my name when I told him he had the right to know something about the person who was going to make sure he lost his license.

Juan ran after me into the station. He wanted a tip. I gave him one over my shoulder.

"If it looks like rain, Juan, carry an umbrella."

We got into the station just as the announcement was being made. The train was running three hours, maybe more, behind schedule.

Everybody in the station, except Juan and me, moaned.

"I told you not to worry mister Joe," Juan said, his smile back in place.

It wasn't until later that I found out why the Sunset Limited was hours late getting into San Antonio.

"We hit a car after leaving Los Angeles," an Amtrak attendant told me as I settled into the seat in my sleeping compartment.

"It happened in Pomona," the attendant said. "A car was stalled on the tracks. Nobody got hurt, but the car was totaled. We had a little damage and had to change engines."

I thought of the retired Amtrak engineer I was riding with the other day. He was telling me that kind of thing isn't uncommon.

"This one had a strange twist, though," the attendant said. "The car was stalled out over one set of tracks. The driver got out and pushed and got it hung up on the second set of tracks. That's the track we were on. If he had left the car where it was, we wouldn't have hit it. Some people can't do anything right."

I'll give you odds that Juan has a brother living in Pomona.

Joe Kelly

The Chicken Man Graces French Quarter

New Orleans, LA -- Prince Keeyama, owner and operator of the Chicken-Man House of Voodoo, was showing me around his establishment, which is in the French Quarter.

I asked how the shop got its name.

Keeyama said he was called the Chicken Man because he would bite the head off a live chicken during voodoo rituals.

I should have known.

Keeyama, 51, was born in Haiti and has been doing voodoo since age 7, he said.

"My grandmother and grandfather taught me everything I need to know."

The prince's shop is small, but he said it contained everything one would want in a quality voodoo store, including $5 autographed photographs of the prince, and chicken feet bones for the same price.

"The feet bring good luck and fast money."

Near the front door is a "wish box". It works the same as a wishing well, except you put in folding money instead of coins. Keeyama takes it from there, literally and figuratively.

I asked the prince what he had in stock to bring me good fortune.

"You'll want a gris-gris bag," he said, which is a red velvet pouch containing herbs, mojo seeds, a penny, dime and quarter.

A gris-gris bag sells for $25. Keeyama was right. The bags do bring good fortune, at least to one person.

By the way, customers have to supply the pennies, dimes and quarters.

Prince Keeyama also does readings.

"I'll tell you about the past, present and future," which takes him 10 to 15 minutes and costs $25.

Hanging around Keeyama's neck are assorted items, including chicken bones, an owl's claw and a monkey paw.

Keeyama held out the monkey paw.

"That's for when you gamble. It brings you money."

In Keeyama's left ear is a quarter. I asked about its significance. Does it keep away bad spirits? Bring good luck?

"It saves me from digging around in my pocket each time I need a quarter."

Oh.

As for voodoo dolls, Keeyama has a variety on hand. I asked if I needed a lock of hair or fingernail clippings or something from the person I wanted cursed.

"I don't need nothing except their name," Keeyama said.

If you only have $10 to spend, consider a "worry doll," Keeyama said. They will cause worry or cure worry, depending on how they are used.

But if a worry doll doesn't cure your worries, there is always the street doctor, who has an office a few blocks away on the curb of St. Peter Street. He'll cure just about everything.

According to his sign, the street doctor cures aches, pains, sore throats, insomnia, hiccups, culture shock, hangovers, sunburn and hysteria, among other things.

"Headaches go away in one to five minutes -- most of them," said the street doctor.

His name is John Baltz, 58, and he claims to work miracles by massaging your neck and shoulders.

"I've learned to sensitize my hands," he said.

The fee for getting your neck and shoulders massaged by sensitized hands is one dollar a minute.

By the way, Keeyama's voodoo shop is on Orleans Street, a few doors off Bourbon Street.

I asked Keeyama, who drives a brand new van, has a beeper on his belt and a Rolex on his wrist, how his voodoo business was doing these days.

Very nicely, he said, especially since splitting from Marie Laveau's House of Voodoo, which is around the corner on Bourbon Street.

There was a dispute, Keeyama said, over how to divvy up the money spent by customers using Master Card and Visa. That's why Keeyama went into business for himself.

"And now when customers go there looking for me," said an upset Keeyama, "they say they don't know where I'm at, but I'm right around the corner."

If your travels should bring you to New Orleans soon, be careful when standing on the corner of Bourbon and Orleans. You might get caught in the crossfire.

There's nothing worse than a voodoo man who is mad at a voodoo woman.

But if you should get hit with a stray curse, there's always the street doctor.

Thoughts From the Train and Stops in Between

Things I've seen, heard and thought while riding around the country on a train:

• Land is at such a premium in San Francisco that it is against the law to have cemeteries in the city. A San Francisco waitress explained it to me this way: "People here are moving to the suburbs just like they are doing in the rest of the country. The difference here is they wait until they die."

• Most graffiti isn't the sort to make note of, but now and then something worth while catches your eye. On a wall near the Los Angeles train station: "Wisdom is knowing what to do next. Virtue is doing it."

• Leon "Whitey" Thompson of San Francisco spent 33 of his 66 years in various prisons, including Alcatraz. He has gone straight since being released in 1975. Thompson's prescription for turning your life around: "Think positive. Stop blaming everybody else for your problems. Rely heavily on the man upstairs."

• Just before the Sunset Limited leaves New Mexico and enters Texas a white post can be seen on the right side of the train. The post marks the Mexican border, just 30 feet away.

• Many of this country's railroad stations look awful. Train travel would be nicer if the stations were. Utica's station is one of the best, far better than what's to be found in Denver, Salt Lake City, Oakland, Detroit, Seattle and other big cities. Los Angeles is lacking in many things, but it does have a nice train station. The train station in Washington, D.C. is probably the best in the country.

• Officially, the cell blocks at Alcatraz, which was once a federal prison in San Francisco Bay, were named A, B, C and D. The unofficial names given to the cell blocks by the inmates were Broadway, Michigan Avenue, Sunset Boulevard and Times Square. The dining hall was called the "gas chamber."

• Give me a quarter for every junk car rusting away within sight of railroad tracks in this country and I could retire. Get the same deal for discarded tires, and both of us could retire.

• When you're lonely late at night and far from home, listening to a train's horn as it goes through railroad crossings in the middle of nowhere does nothing to improve your spirits.

• San Antonio was born in 1718 when a mission was established. The mission was named San Antonio deValero in honor of the Spanish Viceroy, the Marquis deValero.

• Deming, NM, is the site of the world's only duck races, held there every August. I don't think I'll be able to go again this year.

Railroad Saying: 'A Late Train Usually Gets Later'

Aboard the Lake Shore Limited -- I've ridden this train before. The schedule calls for the Lake Shore to get into Utica 45 minutes past midnight and into Chicago at quarter past one the following afternoon.

Because this is an overnight train, I have a sleeping compartment. Trying to sleep in coach is something I can't recommend.

Maybe you've never been inside a railroad sleeping compartment. They come in three sizes: small, smaller and smallest.

Since I am traveling alone and on a budget, I have the smallest. The width of this room will accommodate four hard cover books placed end to end. The room is six foot something long.

Despite its size, it contains a chair, wash basin, toilet, luggage space, shaving mirror, dressing mirror and switches to control temperature and lights. There is a strong lock for the sliding door. At night, the bed folds out of the wall.

Some people don't like a train's rocking motion. I'm usually asleep somewhere between Syracuse and Rochester.

The train, which was 20 minutes late into Utica last night, is now 90 minutes behind schedule. It's 7 a.m. and we are stopped. The sign on the station platform says, ERIE, PA.

Right here I should make an important point. Don't take a train unless you have patience and time. If you have enough of both, I believe you'll enjoy the trip.

There is time to read, time to think, time to dream, time to doze, time to watch the world roll past your window. Unfortunately, it isn't always a pretty sight.

I rub my eyes open as we pull out of Erie, past junkyards, rusting factories, dirty buildings and piles of used 50-gallon oil drums. The view from a train is often the worst a community has to offer, especially in the east.

The dining car is filled for breakfast. As a rule, train food is good. There are exceptions to every rule.

Lake Erie slips by and we pull into Cleveland's station. A waiter has seated me at a table with three woman in their 30s. They are traveling together.

Amtrak dining cars sit four to a table. There are always more customers than tables. Unless you are traveling with a group of four, plan on eating your meals with one, two or three strangers.

That can be wonderful or it can make you want to excuse yourself and carry your plate back to your room.

The women I've been seated with are in the first category. They are personable, polite and talkative. They are returning to Toledo after a long weekend in New York City, a weekend away from husbands and kids.

"We had a great time," Karen Lakis says, which is surprising considering that $100 was stolen from their hotel room, one of several things that went wrong.

"But we want to go back," Shelly says.

"Next time we want to do the museums," Beth says.

The spirit of the American tourist. Or maybe it really is fun to get away from husbands and kids for a weekend.

More time is lost east of Toledo when the train comes to a stop between two fields. Conductors spend 10 minutes checking under the train. They think there might be a loose air brake hose.

A fellow named Chance is chief of onboard services. Chance is his first name. He says he is named after a character in a Tennessee Williams play.

I ask Chance if there's any chance of us making up lost time and getting to Chicago in time to make connections.

"There's an old saying," Chance says, "a late train usually gets later."

At least he's honest.

A couple from New Hartford are on the train. Dick Jordan and his wife, Mary Ann, are going to Chicago, connecting with the Southwest Chief and going to Arizona.

They are on vacation. It's her first train ride. I know this because they are friends of mine.

She says she is enjoying the ride, "but next time I'd like a sleeping car."

So would others. Amtrak could fill more sleepers if it had them, but doesn't have the money to build them.

Chance just announced that connecting trains will be held in Chicago until we get there. That makes the Jordans and many others on this train, including me, quite happy.

In Chicago, though, there will be unhappy people when the delays are announced.

We roll through Elkart and South Bend, getting three-second looks at houses with their backs to the tracks.

We pull into Chicago more than two hours late. I remember what Chance said about late trains usually getting later.

A retirement-age couple gets off the train with me. They had a sleeping compartment in the same car as mine. He is upset about the delay in getting here.

"If we had flown, we'd have been here yesterday," he said.

"Yes, dear," she said, "but we wouldn't have had so much fun."

I swear I saw that gentleman blush.

Joe Kelly

Bumper Stickers

I collect bumper stickers. Not the actual sticker, I collect the messages written on them.

Travel America and you'll see all sorts of bumper stickers, including these:

Electricians are always wired.

Insured by Smith & Wesson.

Love is chemistry. Sex is physics.

Stand on your man.

Engineers know all the formulas.

Pilots are always high.

Bank tellers are well balanced.

Betty Crocker is a flour child.

Nostalgia isn't what it used to be.

Love means nothing to tennis players.

Firemen are always in heat.

I is a college student.

Even paranoids have enemies.

The more I learn about men, the more I like my dog.

Life's too short to dance with ugly men.

She can dish it out, but she can't cook.

When in doubt, worry.

Drink milk -- legal at any age.

Keep your kitchen clean -- eat out.

Pogo sticks make people jumpy.

A Smith & Wesson beats four aces.

I'd rather be 40 than pregnant.

Poets eat rhyme bread.

Honesty is almost always the best policy.

Gun control is hitting what you aim at.

Headaches are all in your mind.

Where Do You "DO IT"?

Bumper sticker messages aren't the only things I collect while traveling. I also collect "do it" messages.

I'm sure you've seen "do it" messages in your travels.

"Teachers do it with class" is one of the more commonly seen "do it" messages. And, of course, there is the ever popular "Beauticians do it with style."

Keep your eyes open. You never know where a "do it" message will pop up.

What follows are some clever "do it" messages, some of which I have even seen:

Artists do it creatively.

Firefighters do it in heat.

Mechanics do it under the hood.

Math teachers do it by the numbers.

Nurses do it with love.

Crafty people do it with their hands.

Race car drivers do it in a hurry.

Baseball players do it in the dugout.

Librarians do it by the book.
Actresses just pretend to do it.
Secret agents do it undercover.
Sprinters do it in seconds.
Painters do it in color.
Stagehands do it behind the curtain.
Singers do it with their mouths open.
Ventriloquists do it with their mouths closed.
Cat burglars do it quietly.
Politicians do it without thinking.
Accountants do it by the numbers.
Diamond cutters do it carefully.
Substitute teachers do it part time.
Marathon runners do it longer.
Musicians do it in tempo
Journalists do it on deadline.

Joe Kelly

Sights, Sounds by the Bay

San Francisco, CA -- There is a rule here requiring visitors to ride the cable cars. So I did.

Along with other tourists following the same rule, I jumped on the running board of the Powell Street cable car, rode it up Jackson and down Hyde, wondering as we went how many vacation pictures I was getting into. People armed with still and video cameras were focused on every cable car in sight.

I rode to the line's end at Fishermen's Wharf, where expensive restaurants are next to McDonald's, where exclusive shops are around the corner from cheap souvenir stands, where the Golden Gate Bridge is to the left and Ripley's Believe It Or Not Museum is on the right.

The U.S.S. Pampanito, a World War II submarine, is docked at Pier 45. Such chances are rare, so I paid $4 and went down a hatch into the aft-torpedo room and from there through the boat.

It was a quick trip. World War II submarines are short, narrow and filled with things to hit your head on.

According to the brochure given out when you board, the Pampanito sank six Japanese ships and damaged four others.

The group in front of me in the forward engine room appeared to be Japanese. One of the men looked to be the right age for World War II.

Mike Lannon, who works for the National Maritime Museum Association, the boat's owner, has charge of the submarine. I asked how many people take the tour.

"On a slow day, 500," he said. "On a busy day, 1,200."

I multiplied those daily numbers by $4.

Maybe the Navy ought to bring the aircraft carrier U.S.S. Oriskany, which is docked in Bremerton, Washington, out of mothballs and start charging admission.

North Beach is a 10-minute cab ride from the wharf. I got dropped at Columbus and Broadway, where Chinese and Italian neighborhoods converge.

Standing there on a small traffic island was a man shouting in Chinese. He yelled in half minute bursts, paused for a half minute and yelled again.

The man kept his hands clasped behind his back and brought them up and down like a bellows, which seemed to generate more force to his words. He wore glasses, a sport coat, sharply creased slacks, open-collared white shirt and looked quite respectable.

I asked the waiter-cook at Cheap Thrills, a carry-out food place, about the yelling.

He laughed and said, "He do that all time."

The waiter-cook pointed his index finger at the side of his head and made a circular motion.

I asked if he knew what the man was shouting.

"I not understand. He Cantonese. I Mandarin."

A few steps from the yelling is City Lights, a landmark bookstore, always open until 11 p.m. It contains books not found elsewhere, including some published by the store.

There are tables and chairs. Nothing is said if customers sit down and read a few chapters.

It was City Lights that got San Francisco to name 12 streets after writers and artists who worked in the city, including Dashiell Hammett, William Saroyan, Jack Kerouac and Ambrose Bierce, the country's first newspaper columnist.

It was near closing when I walked out of City Lights. The Chinese man was still yelling.

I walked over and stood next to him on the traffic island. He ignored me the same as everybody was ignoring him. He went into another burst of yelling. I looked at what he was looking at.

In Saroyan Alley, a man and woman were arguing. He slapped her face. She slapped his. At Big Al's, where lights and signs advertised "Girls, Girls, Girls, Totally Nude, Live," a woman in the open door was puckering her lips at men in passing cars and trying to wave them into the bar. Cars on Broadway were backed up and frustrated drivers were leaning on their horns, which made it difficult to tell where the sirens were coming from. A bearded man, holding a rolled up sleeping bag, asked everybody who walked by for money. Two elderly men at the entrance to Kerouac Alley were drinking something from a paper bag. One got mad when the other took too big a swig.

Maybe the Chinese gentleman has reason to yell.

A Long Way From Home, She's Looking For a Home

Morro Bay, CA -- Meeting Marj and the others happened by accident outside the train station at San Luis Obispo.

They were climbing into a tour bus and heading to Morro Bay, where they would spend the night, and then to Hearst Castle, where I wanted to visit, the next day.

Going with the group was easier and cheaper than renting a car, so I climbed into the bus. The only person to indicate this wasn't such a good idea was a woman who did a quick count and said that with me on the bus there would be 13.

None of the others -- all in their 50s, 60s and 70s -- were superstitious, so I sat in the seat across the aisle from Marj, who also was traveling alone.

"I left home September 6," Marj said as soon as I sat down. "I'm looking for a place to live."

People travel for all sorts of reasons, but Marj, who was starting her fourth week on the road, was the first to give me that reason.

She named several places, including Lake Tahoe and San Francisco, where she had gone looking. So far, though, she hadn't found the right spot.

She said her husband, who did quite well selling televisions, died last Thanksgiving.

"It hasn't been easy," she said, "but you make yourself keep on living. I hate traveling alone, but you've got to do things."

Marj said she and her husband lived near Atlantic City and owned property there and in upstate New York. She doesn't want to live in either place, though.

"Too many memories," she said. "That's why I'm looking for a new place to live."

Marj said she worked for the telephone company for 44 years and retired 15 years ago at 62.

"I've got good benefits, better than what people who work there now get. My husband's medical bills were $197,000. Paying that would have left me broke."

Some travelers tell you personal details about themselves. That's because they don't have to worry about what they say to someone they will never see again. And maybe it's because strangers sometimes listen better than old friends.

The bus pulled into downtown San Luis Obispo, a brief stop for shopping and lunch.

I walked into the Earthling Book Store on Higuera, the main street, and said to the first clerk I saw, "Is this the town where you can't smoke?"

He said, "Smoking is banned in all public places, but there are a couple of bars where the bartenders won't say anything if you light up."

I walked in and out of several commercial establishments, including two bars, checking to see if anyone was smoking. No one was.

Walking on the other side of Higuera was Marj. I wondered what someone looked for when trying to find a new place to live.

By late afternoon we were in Morro Bay, which is part retirement, part fishing and part tourist community.

The tour group was booked into several motels. I had no reservation, so I went into the first one we came to, the La Serena Inn, which is where Marj was staying.

Andy is the manager. He's an older fellow. Judging from a conversation we had over coffee, he's about 80.

Andy, a native of Norway, went to sea early and became a captain at age 31. World War II was on, captains were in demand and Andy joined the U.S. Merchant Marine. It was during the war that Andy met a woman on a blind date.

"We were married two weeks later."

When Andy retired from the sea, he and his wife bought a motel in Virginia. They sold that and managed motels for others until Andy retired a second time.

Andy said his wife died four years ago. Cancer.

"Living alone drives me crazy," Andy said.

Which might be why Andy agreed to come out of retirement and into the La Serena Inn when the owner said he needed Andy's management help.

After dinner, I sat on the patio of a waterfront restaurant. Marj walked by, scouting the town, looking for a place to live.

Later, at the La Serena Inn, I saw Marj again. She was talking with Andy. They were laughing about something.

The next morning the tour group boarded the bus for the short ride to Hearst Castle. Calling it just a castle is an understatement. Anything said about the place built by William Randolph Hearst is an understatement.

We left the castle, stopped in Morro Bay for lunch and then back to San Luis Obispo's train station.

Marj was not with us. She decided to spend an extra day or two in Morro Bay. Maybe she saw something she liked.

I just had a wonderful thought. Wouldn't it be something if Marj, who hates traveling alone, and Andy, who hates living alone, stopped being alone together?

Sitting With Pee-wee, and Other Bad Train News

I've been on fast trains and slow trains, long trains and short trains, clean trains and dirty trains, crowded trains and empty trains, late trains and on-time trains.

Once I even rode a train that arrived early, the Coast Starlight from Seattle to Los Angeles. Even the train's crew was surprised.

"Being on an early train is like getting hit by lightning," one of the crew told me. "It happens, but I don't lay awake nights worrying about it happening to me."

Anyway, as much as I love trains, I hate to see certain things.

Once, for example, on an eastbound train with Billy Butler, the best engineer Amtrak ever had, an 18-wheel tanker truck raced through an unguarded railroad crossing not far from Schenectady.

"You hate to see that kind of thing," Billy Butler said as he watched the truck from the cab of his engine.

According to the instruments in front of Billy, the train was going 80 mph.

"If he stalls that truck on the tracks now," Billy calmly explained, "there's no way we can stop in time."

Since I am able to repeat Billy's words, you can safely assume the truck didn't stall.

That made Billy happy and it made me happy. Had the passengers on the train been able to see the truck clear the tracks, they would have been happy, too.

Not only was it a big truck, I suspect it was carrying some sort of dangerous liquid. I would have hated to see the results of a collision.

These are other things I hate to see while riding a train:

- Masked men on horses riding alongside.
- Being passed by people on bicycles.
- Conductors twirling batons.
- Someone riding shotgun with the engineer.
- Airsick bags on every seat.
- Crying conductors.
- The Lord's Prayer written in dust on a table in the dining car.
- A Pee-wee Herman look-alike in the next seat.
- Sleeping car attendants dressed as clowns.
- Passengers being hand-searched on the way into the dining car.
- A rumble between train personnel and passengers.
- Health inspectors, wearing gas masks and protective clothing, boarding the train during an unscheduled stop in the Nevada desert.

- Anyone wearing a life preserver.
- Yellow "Crime Scene -- Do Not Cross" tape attached to your sleeping compartment door.
- Train personnel garbed in Grateful Dead T-shirts.
- Someone handcuffed to their seat.
- An engineer walking down the aisle carrying a road map in one hand while scratching his head with the other.

Cover Your Ears, Shut Your Mouth and Leave the Train

As much as I love trains, there are certain things even I hate to hear.

It's going to be a bad day on the train if you hear a conductor say any of the following things:

- "Either a steam engine is pulling this train or we are on fire."
- "Are there several doctors onboard?"
- "Ladies and gentleman, you have the distinction of riding on the first train operated by our engineer since his last accident."
- "What made you think this was the train to Chicago?"
- "Believe it or not, this is the first time the club car has run out of beer and liquor at the same time."
- "Don't worry about that trestle. It always shakes when we go over."

- "Everyone, please get down on the floor and cover your eyes."
- "It's only a small fire."
- "This is going to sound worse than it really is."
- "Get your own damn coffee. What do I look like, your servant?"
- "I have good news and I have bad news."
- "Everyone who had the fish for dinner should report to the dining car. Immediately."

Joe Kelly

From 'Smelt Capital of the World' to 'Garlic Capital of the World'

Every community wants to be famous for something. Some communities have more to brag about than others.

Between Seattle and Los Angeles, the route of Amtrak's Coast Starlight, I came across eight communities with unusual claims to fame.

How much fame? You decide.

1. The town of Winlock, about halfway between Tacoma and Portland, claims to be "Egg Capital of the World." They take their eggs quite seriously in Winlock, proven by the egg monument the town has erected in a spot where it can be seen by Amtrak passengers.

2. A few miles down the track is Kelso, the "Smelt Capital of the World." I'm told that in January and February, thousands of the tiny silver fish swim up the Cowlitz River to spawn. I'm not sure if this is a tourist attraction.

3. They say the area surrounding Albany, Oregon, is where 95 percent of the country's grass seed comes from. So next time you're mowing the lawn, think of the people up Albany way.

4. If you're like me, you've probably wondered on more than one occasion about the location of the "Lumber Capital of the World." That honor goes to Eugene, Oregon.

5. Martinez, halfway between Sacramento and Oakland, is where the Martini was invented. It's also the home of baseball great Joe DiMaggio. The street and park named in his honor can be seen from the train.

6. The "Garlic Capital of the World" is Gilroy, just south of San Jose. Every year they have a garlic festival, Gilroy's equivalent, I suppose, to Utica's "A Good Old Summer Time."

7. Be advised that Castroville, Calif., is the "Artichoke Capital of the World." Miles of the bushy plants have been planted parallel to the train tracks.

8. A few miles south of Castroville is Salinas, which calls itself "The Country's Salad Bowl" because of the variety of vegetables grown there.

Three other bits of mostly useless information gathered while riding the Coast Starlight:

- There is a place, just north of San Luis Obispo, where passengers seated in the middle of the train can look out the window and see the Coast Starlight's engine on the right and train's last car on the left. The place is called Horseshoe Curve, an appropriate name.

- The missionaries who founded the mission at San Luis Obispo in 1772 had a problem. The thatched roofs on their buildings kept catching fire. They solved the problem by inventing the red roof tiles that have become a trademark of mission architecture in the West.

- Between Santa Barbara and Ventura, many beaches can be seen from the train. Amtrak passengers seem most interested in Bates Beach. Did I mention that Bates Beach is a nude beach?

Sleuth Searches For Sam Spade

San Francisco, CA -- Fog rolled in from the bay. The night air was chilled. The dark streets were deserted.

I turned up the collar on my trench coat and stood waiting in the dead end alley, where the murder happened all those years ago.

I was following in the steps of San Francisco's greatest private detective, Sam Spade.

Actually, my imagination carried me away there for a second. To be honest, it was rush hour and not yet dark. The sky was clear and I unzipped my jacket because I was warm after the walk from the hotel.

The murder?

Well, that did happen here in Burritt Alley, but only in Dashiell Hammett's mind while writing his classic mystery, "The Maltese Falcon."

If you didn't read the book, you probably saw the movie with Humphrey Bogart as Sam Spade.

One of these days I'll probably get tired of watching "The Maltese Falcon." I expect that will happen right after I get tired of eating and sleeping and riding the train, which is how I got here.

The movie starts with Spade getting a 2 a.m. phone call.

"Hello...Yes...speaking...Dead?...Yes...Fifteen minutes...Thanks."

Spade got dressed, phoned for a cab and was dropped off where Bush meets Stockton, less than 50 steps from Burritt Alley.

By the way, Maltese Falcon devotees have put up a plaque in Burritt Alley. I took out my notebook and wrote down the words.

"ON APPROXIMATELY THIS SPOT, MILES ARCHER, PARTNER OF SAM SPADE, WAS DONE IN BY BRIGID O'SHAUGHNESSY."

I waited in the alley for ages, hoping someone would show interest in the plaque, thus giving me an opportunity to talk with them about Spade and Hammett.

I waited in vain. No one -- except for the woman who illegally parked her BMW -- entered the alley.

Another idea came to me. I walked out of the alley, crossed Bush and turned right on a street once named Monroe. It took less than five minutes to walk up the steep hill to the apartment building at No. 20.

This is where Hammett lived when he created Sam Spade, Brigid O'Shaughnessy, Joel Cairo and Caspar Gutman, and that's why Monroe Street is now called Dashiell Hammett Street.

I looked for a plaque on Hammett's old apartment building. There was none. A woman came out the front door, high heels clicking on the red brick steps, and paused under the awning when she saw me.

I asked if she knew which apartment had been Hammett's.

"Who?"

Dashiell Hammett, I explained, and named the books he wrote in the 1920s and '30s, "The Thin Man," "Red Harvest,"

"The Dain Curse." I told her about the crimes his characters were guilty of and how his detectives brought them to justice.

"Look, I don't know about any of this," she said as she stepped around me. "Talk to the manager."

I picked up the phone next to the front door, pressed the button marked "manager" and asked if he knew which apartment had been Hammett's.

"No," the manager said, "but I'd like to. Do you have any idea?"

At last, someone who knew about Hammett and showed interest.

"How often do people ring the buzzer seeking information about Hammett?" I asked.

"I think you are the first, but on Saturdays a man leads a tour up here and I see them standing out front. I have to go. Dinner is cooking."

I walked down the hill, turned left on Bush, walked several blocks, went right on Kearny, turned left on Sutter and entered the 22-story office building at No. 111.

A man wearing a sport coat and the emblem of American Protective Services got up from his lobby desk and asked if he could help me.

I told him about "The Maltese Falcon." I said Sam Spade and his partner Miles Archer had offices in the 111 Sutter building.

"We don't have any detectives that I know of in this building. This building is owned by Wells Fargo."

Incredible. How could these people live and work here and not know about Spade and Hammett?

Maybe I'd find someone at John's Grill on Ellis Street, where Sam Spade always went for chops, baked potato and sliced tomatoes.

My hunch paid off. The awning outside read "John's Grill, since 1908," and "Home of the Maltese Falcon."

I opened the door and walked inside. It was a little too crowded, a little too warm, a little too noisy. Everything I had hoped.

The barroom was done in dark woods and brass. The dining room had wooden booths and white tablecloths.

On the wall was a picture of Hammett. His biography was on the menu.

Upstairs, in the Hammett Den, were pictures of the movie's stars -- Bogart, Mary Astor, Peter Lorre, Sydney Greenstreet -- and a replica of the Maltese Falcon.

I ordered a dinner that was OK and too expensive. Food, though, wasn't why I came. During dinner, I met two Hammett fans. They called him Dash. We discussed him, his work and tossed trivia at each other while drinking Bloody Brigids.

There was one more stop to make. My new friends said they'd go with me, but I wanted to go alone.

It was after 10 by the time I got there. The fog really was rolling in and the street was, in fact, almost empty.

I turned my collar up against the chilly night air, looked up at the apartment building at 891 Post Street, between Harvey's Dry Cleaning and Grace's Beauty Salon, and wondered which apartment had been detective Sam Spade's.

Amazing Graceland: Elvis' Star Power Still Packs House

Memphis, TN -- The first thing I did after looking through Graceland was to tap a tour guide on the shoulder and ask, "How many people have taken this tour?"

"I don't know what the all-time total is," she said, "but I can tell you between 1,000 and 2,000 people a day visit Graceland."

I had to be sure I heard right. "Did you say between 1,000 and 2,000 a day?"

"Yes, sir," she said. "This house is the second most visited house in the United States. The first is the White House."

"Amazing," I said.

The Graceland tour ends at Elvis Presley's grave, which is always decorated with flowers. According to the attached cards, the flowers come from Elvis fan clubs and individuals.

To a guard near the grave, I said, "I'm surprised flowers are still coming in."

"They arrive all the time," he said. "It never stops."

"Amazing," I said.

I climbed into a van for the short ride down the driveway and across Elvis Presley Boulevard to the shuttle drop-off point, which happens to be where they sell Elvis posters, records, T-shirts, jackets, mugs, plates, guitars, pictures, bumper stickers, dolls and belt buckles. The list is a lot longer, but you get the idea.

In addition to the gift shops, there is the Elvis Presley Automobile Museum ($4.50), the Elvis Presley tour bus ($1), the Elvis Presley airplane tour ($4.25) and the Elvis Presley movie ($1.50).

If you get hungry, there is the Heartbreak Hotel Restaurant. If you can't wait to see your photographs of Graceland, there is a place to get them processed in one hour. If you want to make a recording, there is a studio. And if you want to get those postcards in the mail right away, there is a U.S. Post Office.

Graceland, of course, was Elvis Presley's home. His immense popularity is why so many people pay $7.95 for the one-hour tour of the house and grounds.

I've been an Elvis fan since I watched him on the "Ed Sullivan Show". Those who are old enough to have seen the show might recall that Elvis was only photographed from the waist up. His body movements were too much for television back then.

I'm not one of those Elvis fans who knows every detail of his life. Here are things I didn't know before taking the Graceland tour:

- Elvis played racquetball and enjoyed it so much he had an indoor court, complete with a lounge, built behind Graceland.

- Graceland, built in 1939, is the name given to the property before Elvis bought the house and 13.8 acres in 1957 for $100,000. He liked the name and kept it.

- Elvis made 33 movies. I didn't realize it was that many.

In Elvis Presley's trophy room are some of his awards, which number into the thousands, some of his personal possessions, and a display of quotes from people who knew him.

I like the quote from Dick Clark because it doesn't try to make Elvis Presley more than he was and it doesn't try to diminish what he did.

Dick Clark said: "It's rare when an artist's talent can touch an entire generation of people. It's even rarer when the same influence affects several generations."

The people touring Graceland range from the elderly to youngsters who weren't born until after Presley's death.

There is one more sentence to Dick Clark's quote about Elvis.

"Elvis made an imprint on the world of pop music unequaled by any other single performer."

Even Elvis Presley's critics would have to admit that.

One final note about Graceland. I'm glad I went.

The thing I enjoyed most is the thing I didn't have to go to Graceland to do. For a long time I sat on a bench outside the tour center listening to uninterrupted Elvis Presley music.

To Know The City Of New Orleans Is To Ride It

Aboard the City of New Orleans -- Thanks to Arlo Guthrie, this train is well known.

You've probably heard him sing "City of New Orleans," which has been played on the radio for years.

This being my first time on this famous train, I've decided to check the accuracy of Guthrie's words, which is why I have a tape of his song in my Walkman.

It starts like this: *"Riding on the City of New Orleans...Illinois Central Monday morning rail...15 cars and 15 restless riders...3 conductors, 25 sacks of mail."*

Well, it's Amtrak now, but we are riding on Illinois Central track. We have 10 cars and many more than 15 riders. Nine sleeping compartments in my car are occupied. The coach I just walked through had about 25 passengers. Some looked restless, but then overnight in coach can do that to you.

I've seen two conductors, not three. One of them said no mail was onboard.

"We used to carry the mail," the conductor said, "but we lost the contract. We are hoping to get it back, though."

The song continues: *"All along the southbound odyssey the train pulls out of Kankakee and rolls along past houses, farms and fields...Passing trains that have no names, freight yards full of old black men and the graveyards of rusted automobiles."*

Yes, we are heading south to New Orleans. It's an odyssey, at least for me. The City of New Orleans is one of several trains I've ridden on this 9,200-mile trip around the United States.

There was a stop last night at Kankakee, 57 miles south of the train's start in Chicago. We've been rolling past houses, farms and fields ever since. We are also rolling past towns consisting of one gas station, one store, one bar, one church and a few houses.

Heading north are long freight trains that have no names. I haven't seen any freight yards yet, although I could have missed some while sleeping.

There is no missing the graveyards of rusting automobiles, though. They can be seen from this and every train.

"Dealing card games with the old man in the club car," the song continues, *"penny a point ain't no one keeping score..Pass the paper bag that holds the bottle, feel the wheels rumblin 'neath the floor."*

Club cars on every train have a card game going. The City of New Orleans is no exception. Two games are in progress right now. I haven't seen money change hands, though, not even at a penny a point.

People are drinking in the club car, but not from a paper bag. They are going to the bartender and ordering drinks at not unreasonable prices. Two passengers are drinking fast.

"And the sons of poor men porters and the sons of engineers ride their father's magic carpet made of steel...Mothers with their babes asleep, rocking to the gentle beat and the rhythm of the rails is all they feel."

I don't know anything about the fathers of the people on this train. As for the ride, magic carpets are smooth and this isn't. Trains rock and roll and at times are difficult to walk through.

Sometimes, though, when track conditions are just right, the train takes on a gentle beat. This is especially true at night, but that hasn't stopped a baby back in coach from crying.

"Nighttime on the City of New Orleans, changing cars in Memphis, Tennessee. Halfway home we'll be there by morning, through the Mississippi darkness rolling down to the sea."

We didn't change cars in Memphis. The train arrived there at 5:30 a.m. and departed 10 minutes later.

Yes, Memphis is the halfway point, but New Orleans won't come until 1:40 this afternoon. The schedule must have been different when the song was written.

But all in all, the song captures the spirit of the train it has made famous, and the words are fairly accurate.

And I like the song even better, now that I've ridden the train on which it was written.

Voodoo Master Faces Hard Times Despite Lotions and Potions

New Orleans, LA -- The first thing I did after checking into a hotel on St. Ann Street, in the French Quarter, was to go look up Prince Keeyama.

He is as much a prince as I am a king, but when selling voodoo to tourists, Prince Keeyama is a good name, better than Fred Jones or Bill Smith.

I walked down St. Ann, over Bourbon, and turned onto Orleans. I stopped in front of the small shop that should have been Prince Keeyama's House of Voodoo, but was now occupied by Steve's Framing Shop.

I went in and asked about Keeyama. The person working on frames said nobody by that name ever had a shop there.

I said that was strange considering that I was in the shop last year and watched Prince Keeyama sell potions, lotions, herbs, voodoo dolls and God-only-knows-what else.

"What do you want to know about him?" asked Steve.

At least I assumed I was talking with Steve. I thought it best not to ask.

I told Steve my reason was purely social, nothing important.

"A lot of people want to talk with the Chicken Man," Steve said without looking up from his work.

At this point I should mention that Prince Keeyama is also known as Chicken Man, a title that comes from his practice of biting the heads off chickens during voodoo rituals.

My feeling is that Prince Keeyama would have made it big in professional wrestling had he not opted for voodoo.

Say what you want, Keeyama, 52, is quite the entrepreneur. Last time I talked to Keeyama, he was filling gris-gris bags, "guaranteed to bring good luck," with $1 worth of ingredients and selling them to tourists for $25.

Which happens to be the same price Keeyama charged for the 10 minutes it took him to tell you about your past, present and future.

Steve, if that's his name, didn't want to talk about Keeyama, if that's his name, which it probably isn't.

I told Steve he had several nice prints in the shop, good souvenirs and at reasonable prices, but that I couldn't concentrate on buying anything until I found out about Keeyama.

"Some people say the Chicken Man might be in jail," Steve said.

Steve claimed that was all he knew, which is why I started walking up Orleans in the direction of Jackson Square.

A fellow was sweeping the walk a few doors up from Steve's. I asked if he knew about Prince Keeyama, also known as Chicken Man.

"He's in jail."

Oh?

"They found him with a weapon that had been used in a murder. I don't know what they arrested him for, but they arrested him."

This means more business for Marie Laveau's House of Voodoo, nearby on Bourbon Street, where I went next.

There had been a feud between Prince Keeyama's Voodoo Shop and Marie Laveau's Voodoo Shop. The Chicken Man worked at Laveau's shop until branching off on his own.

Laveau's small shop was crowded. The first thing that caught my eye was a sign. "We do remove hexes," it read. That information could come in handy.

I would have talked with the woman behind the counter except she was busy taking care of a Master Card customer.

There is much to select from at Marie Laveau's. The shop has herb packets containing orris root, carried to attract the opposite sex; quassia chips, burned to render you and your lover inseparable; beth root, worn around the neck for good luck; and Guinea pepper, used to break up marriages.

A total of 50 voodoo mixtures are sold at Marie Laveau's, including galangel. Voodoo people say carrying galangel into court will get you a favorable verdict.

I can't help but wonder if Prince Keeyama has a good supply of galangel on hand.

Joe Kelly

Encounters Of The Nice Kind

Travel and you meet people. The more you travel, the more people you meet. I've met many.

This is my question: How come some strangers remain in your memory and others are forgotten?

Don't ask me because I don't know.

I do know this, though. When you make contact with someone while traveling, it will most likely be the first and last meeting. The parties involved know that their conversation must be direct because the time is limited.

You tell me your story, I'll tell you mine. Usually both stories are honest. There is no reason to lie.

Tracy Taylor is one of the strangers I met. As I said, I don't know why I still remember him.

Taylor, who operates a catering truck, is an entrepreneur. He fills his truck with pastry, sandwiches, candy, juice and cigarettes, and drives to places where people can't get those things. He goes to places such as factories, construction sites and the Amtrak station in Salt Lake City, where he arrives before the sun is up and stays for about an hour.

Outside the Salt Lake City train station is where I met him one dark morning. I didn't need anything he was selling, but when going cross country on a train, a breath of fresh air is always welcome.

So I stood outside and watched him make an announcement as he walked through the station.

"Buy one cup of coffee and get free refills. Right outside."

That policy cost him on the day I was there. Salt Lake City is where three eastbound trains meet and join. One was late and the other two had no choice but to wait, meaning there was plenty of time for refills on the coffee. I had three.

"This is a great place," Taylor said of the station. "You meet such fascinating people. I enjoy people. I enjoy talking to them."

Taylor, age 40, is originally from Dallas. He is a religious man, the father of five, and has been operating a catering truck for 19 years.

I asked if it was difficult making a living.

"My dad told me a long time ago it isn't how much money you make in life. The important thing is whether you enjoy life. I'm my own boss. I'm doing what I enjoy."

Taylor is making enough to put his children through college. One is an honor student.

If life ever puts you at the train station in Salt Lake City, go outside and get your coffee from Taylor instead of from the vending machine. Taylor's is better and you get free refills.

On the Desert Wind, which was parked on the tracks a hundred yards or so from Taylor's catering truck, was a woman named Beth Hodge. My guess was that she, like most of the train, was still asleep.

The day before, I sat across the lunch table from Beth Hodge. She said she was a private detective. Jobs are one of the first things people ask about when they meet. She said she was a Los Angeles private detective.

I'd have been disappointed had she been from any other city. A detective from Toledo, Ohio wouldn't impress me much.

Actually, she is a retired private detective, surprising since she looked to be in her 40s.

"I had enough," she said. "It was time to move on. But I was pretty good at it. People aren't as suspicious of a woman. They tend to open right up."

I'd certainly tell Beth Hodge more than I'd tell some guy with a beer belly and a smelly cigar in his mouth.

People are even less suspicious of two women, Hodge said, which is the reason she often took girlfriends along on jobs.

Hodge has been married twice. She divorced her first husband, an alcoholic.

"Sometimes you just have to say enough is enough. I'm very happy now."

As for her first husband, "He's dead now," she said. "The drinking killed him."

She was traveling alone. I didn't ask the whereabouts of her second husband.

She said she was looking to start another career. She wasn't sure what. Unlike most other people I know in their 40s, she didn't seem at all concerned about starting over.

Those are two people I encountered on a trip once. Why they remain in my memory, I do not know.

Beverly Hills: Home Sweet Home

Hollywood, CA -- Being here offers a rare opportunity to see movie stars as they really are. It's one thing to see them on the screen, quite another to see them at home mowing the lawn, taking out the garbage or washing the family car.

So I climbed into a van with eight other people and let a tour guide show us where the stars live.

We departed from Hollywood and Vine and drove along the Sunset Strip. We went past a restaurant owned by Elton John, past the dress store owned by Priscilla Presley, past the restaurant once frequented by Marilyn Monroe, past the place Tom Cruise goes for hamburgers and past the motel where John Belushi did himself in with drugs.

We didn't see anybody famous at any of those places.

We headed to Beverly Hills. I knew it was a place for rich people as soon as we got there. The first house I saw had a four-car garage. The doors were open. Inside were two Rolls Royces, one Caddy and a Lincoln Continental.

"Who lives there?" I asked.

"Nobody important," said the driver.

Oh.

At 720 Maple Street is the beautiful home owned by George Burns. It has to be worth a million dollars, modest by Beverly Hills standards.

A few doors away on Maple is Herb Alpert's house, which looks more expensive. I remember reading he got started by practicing the trumpet in an old garage.

Roxbury Street is lined with palm trees and movie star homes. Within a few doors of each other live Polly Bergen, Rosemary Clooney, Agnes Moorehead and Peter Falk, who has purple curtains in the front windows.

Holmby Hills is the really high-rent district.

"That house right there went for $4 million" said our driver, "and that one there went for $5 million and that one is worth $18 million."

I had to take his word on the last one. Where I come from there aren't too many $18 million homes.

The strange thing is that the person who spent $18 million on the house then spent hundreds of thousands to hide most of it behind a fence, trees and bushes, which is the way it is with many houses here.

Take, for instance, Barbara Striesand's house on Carolwood Drive. You can see the driveway, but that's all.

Also on Carolwood is Rod Stewart's house. I couldn't help but notice the razor ribbon on top of his high fence.

We left Holmby Hills and entered Bel Air.

"This is where the really rich live," said our driver.

"The people in Holmby Hills didn't look poor," I said.

At 700 Nimes Road is Elizabeth Taylor's house. The house was hidden from view, but I saw a basketball net in her driveway, which surprised me. I can't picture her taking a jump shot.

A couple streets away is a brick house belonging to Tom Jones.

Around the corner is the house used in "The Beverly Hillbillies." The house is being renovated. Much of the construction work is hidden by tarps.

"People around here like their privacy," said the driver.

A minute from there is the house used in the movie "9 to 5". A happy looking man and woman were walking across the lawn, probably looking for an out of place blade of grass.

The driver said something which explained why the couple looked so happy.

If the exterior of your house is used in a movie, as their house was, you get paid $1,000 a day. If the interior is used, as their house was, you get $3,000 a day.

We rode back into Holmby Hills and stopped in front of Hugh Hefner's Playboy Mansion. To gain entrance, you speak into a microphone embedded in a rock next to the driveway gate. A television camera is trained on the rock.

The most expensive house on the tour was saved for near last. Producer Aaron Spelling lives on a hill in a new mansion worth $52 million.

Two trucks with "air conditioning repair" written on the sides were at a back entrance. For $52 million, you wouldn't think there would already be problems with the air conditioning.

I asked the driver if he ever saw stars.

"All the time. Not long ago I saw Jimmy Stewart and Tom Cruise, and I just handed a script to Shirley MacLaine."

Our driver, who has a sign on his van's visor stating "All Tips Appreciated," wants to be a writer.

When I got out of the van, I gave him two tips: a one dollar bill and I told him to forget about writing and go to acting school instead. They are the ones making all the money.

I never did see a movie star mowing the lawn, taking out the garbage or washing the car.

I did see one celebrity, though. Polly Bergen stepped out of her gray house, slipped behind the wheel of her gray Mercedes and waved.

Which is more than I would have done had I walked into my driveway to see a van full of gawking, picture taking tourists.

In Las Vegas, The Customer Always Comes First

Las Vegas, NV -- The people here are quite helpful.

They have, for example, constructed the Amtrak station so that it leads directly into the Union Plaza Hotel and Casino, meaning train passengers can start gambling within 120 seconds after leaving the train, quicker for those who run, which many do.

In fact, the inside of the Union Plaza is as much of Las Vegas as some train passengers ever see. The following story was told to me by an Amtrak employee on the Desert Wind.

There are these two women, he said, who live in Los Angeles and travel together to Las Vegas on the Desert Wind once a month. One is a factory worker. The other owns her own business. Both are married, but they make the Saturday trip without husbands.

"They walk directly from the train," he said, "into the casino and do nothing but gamble until it's time to take the train back to L.A. on Sunday."

The Amtrak employee also said it was not uncommon for people with destinations other than Las Vegas to get stuck there. The Desert Wind makes a 15-minute stop in Las Vegas and some people can't fight the temptation to run into the casino.

"The train is pulling out and they are still in there trying to get in one last bet," the Amtrak crew member said. "We leave them. I've seen it happen."

The passenger is then stranded without luggage until the next train comes through the following day.

"There was a time when a woman left her kids on the train and ran inside to make a bet. She lost track of time and got left there without her children and without her luggage."

That story was told to me as the Desert Wind approached Las Vegas. While still several minutes away, several announcements were made on the train's public address system about the risk of leaving the train and going into the casino.

One announcement went something like this: "If Las Vegas is not your final destination, but you decide to go into the casino during our brief stop here, we suggest you bring your luggage with you."

After a weekend in Las Vegas, I have other examples of how helpful they are to visitors.

Let's say you are in the casino and get thirsty from all that gambling. You don't have to move. Whatever you want to drink will be brought to you.

They don't even charge for drinks, although you are expected to tip the scantily clad woman who delivers it to you. In fact, you are expected to tip everything that moves in Las Vegas, even if they are wearing lots of clothes.

Now let's say you get hungry and go to eat. A helpful casino worker will come to your table and accept your keno bets during dinner.

I was sitting next to a couple in a casino restaurant. They lost $100 before they got to the dessert.

You don't have to worry about running short of money, though. Machines in the casinos will accept your credit card and give you cash.

If your credit card is maxed out, you can go to Western Union, which never closes, and wire home for money.

As I said, people here are very helpful.

Now let's say you get really crazy and decide to get married. They make that easy, too. There is no waiting, no blood test, nothing to do except pay $27 for a license, which happened 75,002 times last year.

They even have wedding chapels that take care of everything, including rings, pictures, flowers, photos, cars, music and wedding gown rental.

I spent most of my time in Las Vegas playing slot machines. It's possible, I discovered, to go through a $10 roll of quarters in less than six minutes, and I wasn't even trying hard.

There never was a need to worry, though. A helpful woman always was close at hand to sell me more quarters.

The only other gambling I did was at the roulette table. I made a few small bets while sitting next to a gentleman making $100 bets. At one point, he bet $1,000 on number 17, the same number I was playing for $5.

We lost. I took it hard. He accepted a drink from a helpful cocktail waitress, smiled and went back to making $100 bets.

Yes, people in Las Vegas are quite nice to visitors.

I'm leaving town now. I can't afford to let them keep helping me.

'City of Angels' Isn't Heaven to Everyone

Los Angeles, CA -- If I were to send you a postcard from downtown Los Angeles, it would read, "Be glad you aren't here."

If I were to send you a postcard from Rodeo Drive -- the exclusive shopping district -- it would read, "Increase limit on credit card before coming here."

The Rodeo Drive shopping area, I was surprised to learn, is only two blocks long, soon to be three. The street itself is much longer, but it's residential.

The shops are even more exclusive than I thought. I entered a jewelry store to browse and was confronted by an arrogant clerk.

"Do you have an appointment, sir?"

Which I didn't, so I left and went into a men's clothing store. An appointment wasn't needed, but an armed guard followed me around the store until I left.

Maybe the people on Rodeo Drive were put off by my appearance. Granted, I hadn't shaved in a week, and my T-shirt and shorts were wet with sweat, but that happened because I ran four miles to Rodeo Drive to get exercise and to avoid the high price of a cab.

I'm not upset, though. If I hadn't been made to feel so unwelcome on Rodeo Drive, I might never have gone to Hollywood Boulevard to look at the prints made by the feet and hands of famous people, prints which have been preserved in cement in front of Grauman's Chinese Theater.

By the way, when Clint Eastwood was asked to sign his name and put his prints in cement, he did, and he added this: "You made my day."

It was while standing in the prints left by Clint Eastwood that CBS asked for my help. A network representative approached me and said CBS was interested in my opinions about its television shows.

"Knowing what you like and dislike will help us determine whether to put a show on the air or what needs to be done with a show already on the air."

I was flattered.

"All that's required is an hour of your time."

I said there was no way I could give them an entire hour.

"CBS would like to give you a free gift for participating."

A free gift? What kind of free gift?

"That changes from time to time. I'm not sure what they are giving out now, but it's something nice."

I said I'd be happy to cooperate. Hey, if CBS needed my help, how could I refuse?

Besides, it wouldn't be fair to complain about CBS programming later if I refused to help them now.

"Where," he asked, "are you from?"

I told him and asked why he wanted to know.

"We aren't including local people in our market research."

Based on my short time looking around L.A., I could understand the wisdom of that decision.

I walked across Hollywood Boulevard into the Roosevelt Hotel and up to the second floor screening room. There were 15 of us and we were each shown to a desk equipped with two cables.

A woman introduced herself, said she was our program director and had us fill out a form, which asked questions about age, education, hometown and job. I'm still not sure why I said I was a professional rodeo clown.

She had us take the cable with the green button in one hand and the cable with the red button in the other.

"When you see a segment you like, press and hold the green button for as long as you enjoy what you are seeing. If you don't like a segment of the show, press the red button and hold it as long as that's your feeling. If you are indifferent, don't do anything."

She asked us to sit through the entire 60 minute show without talking. Actually, it was less than an hour because there were no commercials.

We were shown an upcoming program of "The Trials of Rosie O'Neill," a series already on the air, starring Sharon Gless.

I recognized her as soon as the program started. She was one of the stars in "Cagney and Lacy", although I don't know if she was Cagney or Lacy.

In any event, her old series was better than her new one. My left thumb is still sore from holding down the red button.

I gave the woman at the next desk a thumbs-down sign. She nodded her head in agreement and went back to writing postcards.

The woman next to her was doing her nails and the man she was with was resting his eyes.

When the show ended, each of us got another form. One question asked what we liked best about the show.

I wrote "lack of commercials."

They didn't permit talking in the viewing room, but a few of us got together later in the hall and compared notes.

One woman said she loved the show, but I believe she was drunk. Anyway, her opinion won't help the show. She got the cables mixed up and pressed the "dislike" button when she meant to be pressing the "like" button and didn't realize her mistake until the show was nearly over.

Her positive opinion, according to my informal survey in the hall, was in the minority. Comments ranged from "no good," in the opinion of the guy who slept through it, to "not very exciting," which is what the lady who spent the hour writing postcards said.

So, if "The Trials of Rosie O'Neill' is taken off the air, thank me and my fellow reviewers.

As for the free gift we were promised, each of us received a plastic CBS key chain that turns into a pen. In other words, CBS gave us an item worth a dollar, maybe two, for helping them make multi-million dollar programming decisions.

That brings to mind an old saying, "You get what you pay for."

When You See Elvis, It's Time To Go Home

Aboard the Crescent -- The next stop is Baltimore, which won't come until tomorrow. I can't wait.

It isn't so much wanting to be in Baltimore as it is wanting to be home. Baltimore is only 185 miles from New York City, which is only 237 miles from Utica and home.

This trip has covered 10,000 miles. By airplane that isn't much, but I've been riding a train and it's time to get off and go home.

How do I know this? There are several ways.

It is time to get off the train and go home when:

- You can't remember your home telephone number.
- You miss going to work.
- You invite the conductor to your room for a game of chess, even though you don't know how to play chess.
- You look out the window and think you see Elvis standing at a railroad crossing in Slidell, LA.

- You mess up a perfectly made bed just so the sleeping car attendant will come back and talk to you again while making it.
- You start to enjoy whistling.
- You adjust the sleeping compartment light and make shadow puppets on the wall.
- You send "wish you were here" postcards to people you don't even like.
- You offer to assist the dining car staff.
- You think you saw Elvis standing at a train crossing in Tuscaloosa, AL.
- You read "Express," Amtrak's complimentary magazine, for the fourth time.
- You try to teach yourself to yodel.
- You make a list of your friends and rate them on a scale of 1 to 10.
- You offer to conduct CPR classes in the club car.
- You snap pictures of everyone who waves at the train.
- You decide to see if the emergency exit window really works.
- You think you saw Elvis standing at a railroad crossing near Atlanta, GA.
- You try to goad the nuns in the compartment next door into a balloon fight.
- You start counting junk cars along the tracks.
- You stand in front of the mirror trying to imagine what you'd look like without a mustache.
- You use algebra to figure out how many railroad ties there are in 10,000 miles of track.

- You rewrite the operating instructions for Amtrak's toilet.
- You think you saw Elvis standing at a railroad crossing in Spartanburg, SC.
- You make a list of every railroad song ever written, and start singing them on the train's public address system.
- You use your T-shirts to make window curtains.
- You rearrange the contents of your wallet.
- You know more about the conductor's family than you can remember about your own.
- You send thank you notes to train crew members and invite them over for dinner the next time they are in Utica.

But the best way of knowing it's time to get off the train and go home is when you sit in your sleeping compartment putting together a list of the reasons why it's time to get off the train and go home.

Best Part of Traveling? The Beginning and the End

Aboard the Lake Shore Limited -- With the exception of being mugged, getting sick on restaurant food or drinking too many Hurricanes, which is the drink of choice when in New Orleans, my greatest fear during this trip was oversleeping in some hotel and missing my train.

Oversleeping on the train wasn't as much of a worry, though. They have a good system, much better than the way it's done in hotels.

Before retiring for the night, you give your wake-up time to the sleeping-car attendant. The next morning he or she comes to your room and pounds on the door until you speak at least two coherent sentences.

I think you will agree this is better than having someone call you on the telephone and hang up when you grunt. At some hotels, a machine calls you so it doesn't even know if you grunt.

And some sleeping car attendants, bless them, will even return with coffee to make sure you haven't gone back to sleep.

Who wakes up the sleeping-car attendant is something I've always wondered about.

Oversleeping in a hotel is another matter, and I worry about it all the time. What if they forget my wake up call? What if after they call I decide to close my eyes for just one minute?

Excepting Chicago, where I was on the train a full 90 seconds before it started moving, and Denver, where the train actually was moving when I jumped on, I haven't come close to missing a train on this trip.

Until Baltimore.

My train, or what should have been my train, left Baltimore at 9 a.m. I woke up in the Best Western Hotel on Howard Street, a 20-minute drive from the station, at 9:31.

The front desk claims to have called me at 6 a.m. as instructed. I don't even remember grunting.

Which is why I telephoned Amtrak.

"Stop sobbing," said the Amtrak agent on the other end of the phone. "There is a train leaving Baltimore at 10 o'clock. If you can make that train, it will get you to New York City with just enough time to catch a connecting train that will get you into Utica at 6:09 tonight.

The agent may have said more. I don't know. I was packing.

I am especially proud of the following accomplishment. I was dressed, packed, checked out of the hotel and into a cab by 9:44.

The cabbie must not have known it was supposed to take him 20 minutes to get to the station because we got there in 12.

As I look back on it, maybe the large denomination bill I was waving as I leaned over the front seat had something to do with his speed.

Whatever, cutting through a corner gas station to avoid a red light and going up on a sidewalk to get us out of a traffic jam was especially enterprising on his part.

The cabbie was Russian. He has lived in this country for only a short time. He is learning fast, though. I especially liked his comment when I climbed out of his cab.

"This is a great country we've got here," he said, pushing a large denomination bill into his jeans.

I used the same money waving technique on the cabbie from India who picked me up at New York's Penn Station and got me to Grand Central just in time to catch the Lake Shore Limited.

The New York cabbie wasn't taking a chance, though. He took the bill from my hand at the start of the ride. He has lived here longer than the Russian cabbie.

I'm glad I didn't miss the Lake Shore because it was on that train that I met Tom Dunn, a young man dressed in denim.

"I'm traveling around the country by train," he said in an enthusiastic voice.

We were heading north along the Hudson River.

Trying not to sound too matter of fact, I said I had traveled around the country several times by train. In fact, I was just returning from a long trip.

As you might guess, the young man was interested in my opinions.

"Which train was your favorite?" he asked.

I was able to answer without giving it any thought whatsoever.

"The California Zephyr, Chicago to Oakland," I said.

"Because of the views?"

"No," I said, "because of the crew's fast reflexes. Anybody who can keep an 80 mph train that I'm riding on from smacking into a cement truck, which has stalled at a railroad crossing, is operating my favorite train."

Tom Dunn asked if I had any advice for someone just starting a long trip.

I had two pieces.

"Get yourself a good alarm clock and always carry a large denomination bill."

To order additional copies of Joe Kelly's *Travels in America* book or *Joe Kelly's Greatest Ever Little Trivia Book*, fill in the following form and mail to:

Good Times Publishing
P. O. Box 4545
Utica, NY 13504

Qty	Item	Each	Total
______	Joe Kelly's Trivia Book	$ 9.95	____________
______	Joe Kelly's Travel Book	$12.95	____________
		Sub Total	____________
New York State residents Add 8% sales tax			____________
Shipping & handling for first book: $2.00. Add $1.00 for each additional book			____________
		Total	____________

Make check or money order payable to:

Good Times Publishing

_____ VISA ______ MASTERCARD

Exp Date:______________Card #______________________

Signature: ____

NAME:____

STREET:____

CITY:_______________________________________

STATE:_____________ ZIP CODE________________

Please allow 4 to 6 weeks for delivery.

TRAVEL NOTES:

TRAVEL NOTES:

TRAVEL NOTES:

TRAVEL NOTES:

TRAVEL NOTES:

TRAVEL NOTES:

TRAVEL NOTES: